MAKING A WAY
OUT OF NO WAY

My African American Life

By

Arnold T. Grisham

PEGASUS BOOKS

Pegasus Books
8165 Valley Green Drive
Sacramento, CA 95820
www.pegasusbooks.net

First Edition: January 2024
Published in North America by Pegasus Books. For information, please contact Pegasus Books c/o Marcus McGee, 8165 Valley Green Drive, Sacramento, CA 95823.

Library of Congress Cataloguing-In-Publication Data
Arnold T. Grisham
Making a Way Out of No Way/ Arnold Grisham – 1st ed
p. cm.
Library of Congress Control Number: 2020952557 - TBA
ISBN – 978-1-941859-92-6

1. BIOGRAPHY & AUTOBIOGRAPHY / African American. & Black 2. BIOGRAPHY & AUTOBIOGRAPHY / Business. 3. BUSINESS & ECONOMICS / Banks & Banking. 4. BIOGRAPHY & AUTOBIOGRAPHY / Cultural, Ethnic & Regional / African American & Black. 5. LITERARY COLLECTIONS / American / African American & Black

10 9 8 7 6 5 4 3 2 1

Comments about *Making a Way out of No Way* / and requests for additional copies, book club rates and author speaking appearances may be addressed to Arnold T. Grisham via e-mail to grishama@gmail.com
Also available as an eBook from Internet retailers and from Pegasus Books

Printed in the United States of America

Dedication

I dedicate this book to my mother, Gladys Louise Grisham. My mother spent years in Chicago, putting linings in fur coats for $80.00 a week, but she somehow took me on vacations and exposed me to a larger world through her lens and her love of books. At night, she read to me or had me read to her until she could no longer stay awake. She valued me in a way that caused me to not allow anyone this side of creation define me.

She was gentle with me, and she taught me to be gentle with others. She was as nonjudgmental as a person could be, and she encouraged me to follow her example. She introduced me to her God, and through her teachings, I have been a lifelong follower of Christianity.

I am who I am because of my mother. She transitioned a few weeks before her 95th birthday. She continues to be my North Star. I think about her, and I miss her every day.

In *Making a Way Out of No Way*, Arnold Grisham chronicles the most significant and impactful people and moments in his life that guided his meteoric prominence and influence in California banking. Grisham's early childhood was a period of quietly looking, listening and learning from the people he loved and respected, and feared and longed for love.

With that understanding, empathy and self-awareness, Grisham was blessed during his banking career to be surrounded by a community of African American professionals and thought leaders that changed the world. Arnold Grisham's life and career is a promising story and serves as a model on how we can thrive to make the world a better place.

Teveia R. Barnes
Former and First African American and Woman Commissioner of the California Department of Financial Institutions
Former and First African American and Woman Executive Director of California Infrastructure and Economic Development Bank

———————————

Being "self-made" is not nearly as interesting or admirable as a person from Chicago's South Side who can see the small blessings that came his way with gratitude. He never stopped building community banks to help communities like his, and then grew determined to give back to others having the same challenges he once knew.

Father Dennis Holtschneider, CM
Former President of DePaul University and current President of the Association of Catholic Colleges and Universities

———————————

Arnold Grisham is a kind man and a banker. This superb memoir reveals how both things can be and are true.

George Strait
George was the senior communications executive and has held senior executive positions at the FDA, The National Institutes of Health and the University of California, Berkeley, and he was a television journalist for 30 years, 23 of which at ABC News.

MAKING
A WAY OUT
OF NO WAY

MY AFRICAN AMERICAN LIFE

Making a Way Out of No Way

Table of Contents

Foreword by Michael A. Lenoir
Preface by Arnold T. Grisham

Epilogue

Foreword

Michael A. Lenoir, MD

More often than not, successful people forget their roots. They attribute their success in life to a set of skills that they brought to life's table and an innate ability to succeed. They forget where they started and who helped them along the way. Arnold Grisham is not such a man.

From humble beginnings on Chicago's South Side, Grisham has taken the path of hard work and ingenuity from segregated classrooms to the doorsteps of corporate America. He is one of America's most important financial figures. But he has not forgotten how he got there. Grisham credits the mentors and advisors present in his early years for helping him transcend a working-class background and achieve success. He believes that having relationships with people who can provide guidance and support is essential in achieving personal growth.

This book is not only an enjoyable read as we follow Arnold's life journey, but it is also a treatise on how to manipulate the professional maze. Perhaps most importantly, this memoir represents a masterclass on how to weave family and fortune into a fabric that his peers can appreciate and is a road map for young people to follow.

Preface

From Chicago to Oakland – My Soul looks back in wonder.

Until the lions have their own historians, the history of the hunt will always glorify the hunter.
~Zimbabwean Proverb

Why am I writing this book? I did not want my stories to be lost with the millions of stories that are never told because of all the reasons that stories are not told. The fire in the belly to write this book comes from years of watching others try to define those around them from their own experiences and prejudices. Also, it is important to tell your story while you can, because none of us has as much time as we think, and we never know when we have said our last prayer or had our last meal.

My story is not a single story, but a series of connected narratives, woven together into one life. I have been carrying these stories around for a long time. They have become too heavy to bear. As Alice Hoffman said, "Once you know some things, you can't unknow them. It's a burden that cannot be given away."

I believe that when a person begins to peel the onion of their story in the form of a memoir or autobiography, the author is confronted with a defining question: How much of their truth do they want to share? As a writer begins to write, the details of life can come flooding back like a tidal wave. With each crest and ebb, the author faces the question of what to reveal, what details serve useful purposes and what details need to remain hidden.

So the world has conspired to help me write this memoir, and many are waiting to see if I really want to tell my story. I think I have captured most of my truth, and it is my hope that my story will help me meet my "purpose of life" test.

As I discuss in my "Enjoy the Journey Speech" (Chapter 9), I believe the purpose of life is to change the world. I believe that opportunities to change the world come when other people come into your world, and the trajectory of their life changes in some positive way because of something that you do or say, and then they go on to do something world changing. This is a serious life, and we never know who is watching and who might have a course correction because of our positive examples.

I came to this understanding when a group of Coro Fellows, a select collection of businesspersons focused on training and mentoring community leaders, visited me when I was running a commercial banking group for Wells Fargo in Oakland, and one young intern asked me, "Mr. Grisham, how do you change the world?"

She pulled an answer out of me that I did not know was there. I answered that "you change the world by changing yourself and letting your example be an instrument of change."

The world, in conspiring to help me write this memoir, and with providence moving in my direction, has created in me a sense of knowing that this was something I needed to do, so I hope in some way my story will be helpful to a few people.

Chapter 1: Chicago, The West Side – 1946 to 1958

"In order to have a conversation with someone, you must reveal yourself." ~James Baldwin

The Way begins… Lawson Elementary School

My earliest memories of Chicago include Lawson Elementary School, a public school located at 1236 S. Homan Avenue, in the Lawndale community area of Chicago, Illinois. Visually, Lawson Elementary was dreary and physically imposing. The gray walls and small windows made it look more like a prison than a school. The principal and teachers were strict and no nonsense. Discipline was simple and direct. For instance, a scuffle with another student on the playground resulted in having to report to the basement of the school at the end of the school day, where a boxing ring had been erected. There, a teacher put boxing gloves on the opposed students and refereed a fight. I recently learned from friends who attended Chicago public schools during the1950s that Lawson was not an outlier. Other schools apparently employed this barbaric practice.

Teaching at Lawson was simple and direct as well. When I was in the fourth grade, my white male teacher gave me the option of either completing my assignments and getting a higher grade, or reading comic books, which he allowed students to bring to class. He did this in an effort to separate serious students from the rest. I tried the comic books option for a couple of weeks, until my mother discovered what I was doing. That ended very quickly and very badly for both me and my teacher, who faced my mother's wrath.

The Lawndale Neighborhood

We lived on the second floor of a two-story walk-up at 1236 S. Spaulding Avenue. I remember the iceman coming down the street with ice for our iceboxes, the insurance man coming to collect weekly 25-cent payments for our small insurance policies, and our doctor coming to our home to make house calls. We had a wood burning stove that had to be fired up in the morning. After I got too close to it one day, my mother treated my burn with cooking grease that she kept in a container on the stove.

Like most city neighborhoods, the streets in Lawndale were our biggest playground. We played stick ball and hide-and-seek. One game was especially problematic. During every spring and summer, the city dispatched mosquito abatement trucks to our neighborhood. As they rumbled up and down our streets, bellowing grey clouds of poisonous chemicals to kill mosquitoes, my friends and I made a game of running behind those trucks and playing in that aerosolized toxic soup. It's no wonder that I had asthma as a child—asthma so severe that I slept many nights under a vaporized tent.

I had more than my share of illnesses as a child. In fact, I had pneumonia and measles at the same time and spent weeks quarantined in an infectious disease ward of a local hospital. I had operations to remove my tonsils and appendix, and I also suffered from chicken pox and whooping cough. These early childhood illnesses, along with allergies, plagued me until I moved to California at age 39. I believed until then that health issues would limit my dreams.

My working-class neighborhood was relatively safe, except for one house on our block, where kids were lured into a questionable home with the promise of candy, and where my parents ordered me to stay away. I could wander all over Lawndale and the West Side of Chicago without worrying that anyone was going to bother me. I remember leaving home in the morning and my parents telling me to be home before the streetlights came on at night. When I was left under the supervision of my grandmother, who we called "Big Ma," she was not as lenient. I had to always be within shouting distance of her call. If she did not see me running toward her after two calls, she would demand that I find her a switch from a tree, and the branch had to be big enough for her to whip me on my bare legs.

I had an older sister who died in childbirth, so I was essentially an only child, which meant that I had my mom all to myself. Much of my time was spent going to libraries: the local Lawndale public library and the main library in downtown Chicago. I checked out books and we watched free movies. We sat on folding chairs and watched the movies on a projector screen. Even though I was still in grade school, I realized that my mother was giving me a special experience that my peers in Lawndale did not have, and I can still remember isolated images of those movies today.

I spent most of my free time participating in the Boy Scouts and our local Lawndale Boys Club. My mother introduced me to scouting and became our troop's den mother. Every year, we marched in Chicago's famous Bud Billiken Parade. Created by Robert Abbot, founder of the *Chicago Defender*, a legendary Black Newspaper, Billiken was a fictional Black good luck figure and mascot for youth groups. The parade and picnic have been held in Chicago on the second Saturday in August every year since 1929. I believe it is still the largest African American parade in the nation. I liked the picnic that followed most of all.

Bud Billiken Parades

The Lawndale Boys Club was a great facility with a dedicated staff. The club introduced us to academics, activities and sports that were not available at our school. The facility had a great pool where I learned to swim. Magazines, like *National Geographic* and board games, including chess, were available to us there. My introduction to chess began a lifelong love affair with the game. I have coached high school chess teams, and I currently serve as a board member and chair of the chess committee for the Mechanics Institute, a private library and chess club in San Francisco, founded in 1854.

John and Gladys

"What is the story that we tell ourselves about ourselves? What is your personal narrative? We are the authors of our stories."
~Susan Pinker, TED 2017

My mother, Gladys Louise Grisham, was a fur finisher. She worked for furriers, putting linings in mink and other kinds of fur coats. My father, John Terry Grisham, was a wallpaper shipping clerk.

My mom was an only child. Her church life was very important to her, and she sang in the choir. My dad's primary outside activity was poker. As a child, I remember how he would disappear for days at a time while on a gambling binge. Once, after losing all his money, he came home, grabbed my "Smokey the Bear" piggy bank, filled with coins, and raced downstairs to rejoin his game. As he ran, my mother screamed, "Don't take the baby's money!" which created a searing memory that is as clear seventy years later as it was when it occurred.

John and Gladys had a tumultuous marital relationship. John did not believe that women should drive, so my mother was "not allowed" to drive. While my mother was a constant presence in my life, my father was not. Rarely did she say anything positive about him. My father never laid a hand on me, physically, but if neglect is a form of abuse, then I can say I was abused by my father. He never spent much time with me. My mother tried to make Dad take me places, but he left with me on Saturday mornings, dropped me off with relatives, picked me up at the end of the day and then took me home.

My mother never missed an opportunity to expose me to new experiences. She read books to me until I could read myself. She constantly supplied me with new reading materials, took me to plays and cultural events, made me participate in church programs, where I had to speak in front of audiences, and she took me on vacations. She even enrolled me in tap dancing lessons, where I performed on stage.

I can only remember one time when my mother judged me harshly. During my formative years, she gave me piano lessons, and at some point, she abruptly stopped. It was not until I was fifty, when I asked her why she stopped. My mother, who had always put me on a pedestal, simply said, "You weren't any good."

As a child, I wondered why my father was so distant from my mother and me. As I grew older, I realized that it was because I was a pawn in the middle of a never-ending and never-resolved "death struggle" between the two of them.

Mom and Dad, Wedding Day Picture

Mom

Me and Mom

The Grishams

The Grishams, for the most part, were very successful. They were not rich, but they were solidly "Black folk" middle class. My dad's father, my grandfather, William Grisham, Sr., was a Pullman Porter. While being a porter on the railroad kept him away from his family for weeks at a time, it was a good paying job, especially for a Black man at that time. He made enough money to buy a nice two-story home near the corner of Warren Blvd and Hoyne Street, on the West Side of Chicago.

William Grisham Sr., My Grandfather

My dad had thirteen brothers and sisters. Only four were alive when I was born, William, Gladys, John and James.

Eddie Merrit
Tommie Russell
William Samuel Jr
Annie Sue (twin to my father, John Terry)
Carrie Lucille
Bertha May

Hazel
Baby Grisham (who died shortly after childbirth)
Louis Trimble
Ernest
Gladys Marie
Jewel
James Warren

My father's siblings and their children succeeded, despite going to segregated schools in Chicago during the 1920s and 30s. William had three children: his daughter, Wilda, worked for the City of Chicago; one son, Paul, was a well-liked local pharmacist on the South Side of Chicago; his other son, Daryl, worked in the meat packing business, eventually becoming President and CEO of Parker House Sausage Company, a famous producer and distributor of pork products to the Black community.

Cousin Daryl was a hard-driving executive and highly sought-after corporate board member. He was a director of Harris Bank and Trust Company, Illinois Service Federal Savings Bank, Independence Bank of Chicago, and Upjohn Company. He was a member of several civic and non-profit boards, including Northwestern University, Lyric Opera, Museum of Science and Industry, and the Lincoln Park Zoological Society. Daryl achieved enormous success despite never earning a college degree.

While my cousin was a well-known, respected community and civic leader, known for his tireless dedication to community organizations, he was less interested in helping and mentoring individuals. Our family always chafed when the community constantly told us what a great person Daryl was, because we knew that he was totally uninterested in us, as we somehow did not meet his standards, economically and intellectually. It seemed Daryl was more interested in helping Black folks as a collective rather than helping Black individuals.

My Uncle James served in the Army in the Pacific during World War II. After the war, he had a successful career as a purchasing agent for a local Chicago West Side distributor of manufacturing materials. James' children were educated in Catholic schools and were also successful. One daughter, Linda, a University of Chicago graduate, received a PhD in Pharmacology from Stanford University in California, and another daughter, Joan, graduated from Loyola University in Chicago and became a K-8 grade teacher. James had twin sons: Robert graduated from Illinois Institute of Technology and had a successful career at AT&T, and Lawrence, who graduated from Northwestern University, earned a master's degree from Spertus Institute.

Lawrence has had a storied career, working as a senior advisor and legislative aide to both Illinois Senator Charles Percy and Chicago Congressman Ralph Metcalfe. Metcalf became famous as an Olympic sprinter in 1936, finishing second only to Jesse Owens. Later in his career, Lawrence worked for one of Barak Obama's closest aides, Valerie Jarret, at The Habitat Company, and he served as Managing Deputy Commissioner for Housing for the City of Chicago. At the time of this publication, Lawrence is Assistant Executive Director/Chief of Staff of the Illinois Housing Development Authority.

John's living sister, Gladys, was a typist for the City of Chicago.

My father was never as successful as his siblings and their families were, and I believe his lack of achievement affected him deeply. It made him insecure. He felt inferior and unworthy, and by extension, he felt that we, his family, were also inferior and unworthy. When I became older, I learned that when he was not gambling, he was spending a considerable amount of time with his brothers and their kids. He wanted to be around people who were successful, and his association with them intimated that he and his family were also worthy of high respect. It was a complex psychology.

Part of his strategy involved the church. My father felt that, as a wallpaper shipping clerk, he did not have professional status in business, so it was particularly important for him to have status in his church. He secretly gave money directly to pastors, hoping that they would pay attention to him. He became the president of our church's ushers board, and in that capacity, I watched him periodically make speeches to his board. He was a self-conscious and nervous speaker. While it was often painful for me to watch, because it fed his inferiority, and worse, he projected that inferiority onto my mother and me.

Families and family relationships are complex. I realize that my memories of my mother are positive, because she exposed me to a love for traveling and books. I realize also that my memories of my father have been mostly negative, because he painted my mother and me with his own sense of inferiority, and he caused me to see the world through his lens. One of the most searing moments of my life occurred after flying back from Oakland to Chicago to pay my last respects to my father as he was transitioning from this life. With days left to live, he opened his eyes and looked at me and said, "You sure are ugly." It took a few sessions on a therapist's couch for me to get past that judgment.

As I said, families are complex; nothing is black and white, since in many ways, I am who I am in part because of my father's many positive examples:

- I remember him never missing a day of work unless he was hospitalized for some serious illness, like prostate cancer.
- He taught me the value of hard work and longevity in employment. When I quit a part-time stock boy job at 16, he looked at me disappointedly and said that I might be forever unsuccessful in holding a job. For the rest of my life, I resisted quitting any position, as I remembered his admonition.
- My father was the patriarch of our family, insisting that we ate at a dinner table every evening.
- He was generous with his time and money; he was a loyal family member and friend, and he was not judgmental about the failings of others.
- On one or two Sundays a month, my father would take my mother and me out to dinner at a local White Castle, and desert at a Tastee-Freez, where we would get vanilla cream cones. dipped in chocolate.
- When I bought my first home in Park Forest, Illinois, in 1971 for $37,500, my father took me aside and said, "Boy, you really stepped out there this time. We hope that you know what you are doing. Your mother and I put a few dollars aside in case you have trouble making that $323.00 mortgage note. With the money we have saved, we may be able to help you for a month or two if you get into trouble, but it is important that you realize that you are on your own." I have been running scared ever since. For most

of my career, I was typically the first one in the office and the last to leave, and I would tell my kids that I did not need a morning alarm clock, because my job woke me up.

"The Southwind" – Nashville and Anniston, Alabama

In the early years, my family periodically visited my father's relatives in Nashville, Tennessee. I remember us taking the "The South Wind," a passenger train from Chicago's Union Station. It was a pleasant ride until we reached the Mason-Dixon line, which historically was a dividing line between free states in the North and slave states in the South. At that point in our journey, the train officials and guards forced us to leave our comfortable accommodations and crowd into the "colored car," where many of us had to stand for hours until we reached our destination.

In Nashville, I remember "colored only" restrooms and drinking fountains. I remember my father taking me to the back of the local five-and-dime store to get me an ice cream cone, because we were not allowed to order at the counter. To prepare me for these trips and to remind me how I needed to act while in the South, my parents told me the story of Emmett Till for what seemed like a hundred times. I remember Emmett Till's body being brought back to Chicago's West Side for his open casket funeral and the lines of mourners who came to pay their respects. His mother wanted to have an open casket service so everyone could see the horror of his murder.

In Anniston, Alabama, my mother's family owned a grocery store and other small businesses. My grandmother and my mother were not privy to my grandfather's finances, so when they went to the bank to settle affairs after his death, local authorities insisted that there was nothing there for them and ordered them to leave. My grandmother, who had a limited education, ultimately left Anniston, virtually penniless.

Chapter 2: Chicago, The South Side – 1958 to 1965

Ryder Elementary School to Burnside Elementary School to Harlan High School

My family moved three times during my middle school and high school years. First, we shared a house with a family at 9405 S. Union. This was in a new development where all the other kids' parents owned their homes. We, however, were renters, sharing a home with another family. Our lack of home ownership singled us out as different. Blacks in that neighborhood were becoming more affluent, so sharing a home with another family meant that we were not among the fast risers. Actually, my dad never wanted to own a home, because he had watched his parents struggle to make their monthly mortgage payments. I do not think he realized that they were building equity that would serve them well after they retired.

My parents moved to Chicago's South Side so that I could receive a better education, and I did. At my first school on the South Side, Ryder Elementary, the teachers were focused on individual achievement and there was nowhere to hide in the classroom. Also, the school gave me my first experience in an integrated environment, with White and Black kids. All my teachers were white and had pianos in their classrooms. During those years, I thought that a musical skill set was required to become a teacher in that environment.

We lived eight blocks from our school, and all the kids on my block rode their bikes there. At about the halfway point was a train crossing, and frequently we could see a freight train in the distance. We needed to race the train to the railroad intersection to get to school on time. Sometimes, we barely beat the train to the crossing. I do not think that we fully understood the price we would have paid for losing that race.

When I was in seventh grade, my family moved from Union Ave. into our own apartment, a two-story walk-up at 8922 South Langley. It was a neighborhood of homeowners and apartment dwellers, but it was more comfortable for me because we were not the only family in the neighborhood who did not own their own home.

In 1958 through 1960, three sporting events captivated my attention, and local folks in Chicago barber shops talked about two of those events for decades. In 1958, John Marshall High School became the first Chicago public school to win the Illinois High School Boys Basketball Championship in 32 years. The team was all Black. They won again in1960, and in both years, they were led by their center, George Wilson and their talented point guard, Eddie "Shaky" Jakes. My mentioning Wilson and Jakes is not meant to diminish the talents of other talented team members.

In 1959, the Chicago White Sox won the American League pennant for the first time since 1919. You were not a real Chicagoan if you could not walk into a barber shop and name every notable member of the team and the position that they played.

- First base, Ted Kluszewski
- Second Base, Nellie Fox
- Short Stop Louis Aparicio
- Third Base, Bubba Phillips
- Catcher, Sherman Lollar
- Left Field, Al Smith
- Center Field, Jim Landis
- Right Field, Jim Riveria
- Starting Pitcher, Wynn (Cy Young Award winner)
- Starting Pitcher Billy Pierce
- Relief Pitcher, Bob Shaw
- Relief Pitcher, Turk Lown

During those years, African American major league baseball players lived in African American communities where the teams were located. That meant we knew left fielder Al Smith and his children.

Also in 1959, my father took me to see a Golden Gloves competition at Chicago Stadium. It was the first time many of us saw Cassius Clay (Muhammad Ali) as he won the Light Heavyweight Championship. We all knew we were watching a special athlete. His feet barely seemed to touch the ground as he danced and pranced around the ring. Indeed, he did float like a butterfly... and with the force of his jabs and punches; he did sting like a bee! The memory is doubly special because it was one of the few times my father took me anywhere.

My neighborhood on Union had a boy scout troop. I immersed myself in everything scouting, and I emerged as the Senior Patrol Leader of my troop. It was my first leadership experience, but it happened because I worked harder than anyone else did. Why did I work harder than others? Because my family rented, and I needed to show that we were just as good as the homeowners. I was still proving to my dad that we were worthy.

John Marshall Harlan High School – The way out

In 1961, I was very privileged to be able to attend John Marshall Harlan High School. The school was only three years old, and everything about the school was new and shiny. The teachers were initiative-taking and expected a tremendous amount from all the students. I loved math, and there were numerous courses available, including solid geometry and probability.

I went to summer school every summer, and I took extra classes during the year. I could have graduated in 3½ years, but I was not in any hurry to leave. Harlan had a program that allowed high school students to take math classes at Southwest Junior College, the local community college. I was able to take a night college algebra class there during my senior year, which helped me create a solid math foundation before entering college.

Chapter 3: DePaul University

"The moment one definitely commits oneself, then Providence moves too. All sorts of things occur to help one that would never otherwise have occurred." ~William Hutchison Murray

As a high school senior, I could not decide where I wanted to attend college. I had the opportunity to attend math educational seminars that were hosted by local colleges and universities, like DePaul because I was in Honors math classes. After spending one day at a DePaul math seminar, I was sold. It is hard to explain, but I just felt DePaul was a good fit for me; albeit an expensive one.

In the 1960s, my father made $110 a week and my mother made $80 a week. Nevertheless, my mother always insisted that I get accepted at a college and send her the bill. During all my college years, they never asked to see my grades; they were so proud that I seemed to be successfully progressing forward with my studies.

I began my college career in January 1965. Back then, you could graduate from high school in June or mid-year in January. I graduated in January DePaul had a North Side campus and a downtown campus. I was a liberal arts major, so my classes were at the North Side campus. I had to travel for over an hour by bus and on the famous Chicago "L" to get to and from school every day.

The student body at the university was segregated and reflected the segregated neighborhoods of the city of Chicago. On the North Side campus, there were no more than 25 African American students. During our time at DePaul, many of the Black students became close and have maintained many of those close relationships for over 50 years.

One reason that I am a banker today is my failure to master French 101. I took Latin in high school, but I could not connect the dots to French. I was so lost that, after a disastrous midterm, my professor told me that he would give me a "C" for the class if I promised to never take another French class again for as long as I lived. He kept his promise, and I kept mine. The school of Business did not require two years of a foreign language to graduate. I took my "C" in French 101 and moved on.

When I started at DePaul, the tuition was $450 per semester. In my junior year, DePaul changed from a two-semester school year to a three-quarter school, and the new tuition was $450 per quarter. The third $450 created a severe financial hardship. My father lost his job during that time, so I dropped out of DePaul for a year and took a full-time job at IBM, and I joined the Illinois National Guard.

My guard unit, the 178th Infantry, was formerly an all-Black infantry unit from World War II that had been retired to guard status. When I joined the unit, it was still more than 90% Black, and it was probably the only Black guard unit from the battalion commander to the lowest ranks. My active guard duty consisted of six months of basic training at Fort Leonard Wood, Missouri. I remember an old sergeant on the base telling me one evening that if I saw a ring around the moon at night, I could expect bad weather the next day. I frequently saw a ring around the moon, and it seemed like the weather was awful every day for six months.

I returned from active duty on April 7, 1968, and Martin Luther King, Jr. was assassinated a few days later. The government called my guard unit for the ensuing Chicago riots, and a few months later, we were called up again in response to the "Days of Rage" riots on Michigan Avenue in front of party headquarters of the 1968 Democratic Convention. When I returned to DePaul in September 1968, I was a very focused student.

While at DePaul, I did not realize how committed DePaul was to its mission, which was to educate young people from working class families in the greater Chicago area. While I was from one of those families, I did not know I was a "mission" kid, nor did I appreciate how committed the priests were to our success, until more than 35 years later, when I was asked to join DePaul's Board of Trustees.

DePaul is a remarkable place. It is the largest Catholic university in the country, but the school had to use its cash flow to grant scholarships and financial aid to deserving students and students in need. I spent nine years as a trustee, and I have been grateful for all the points of intersection that my life has had with DePaul.

One day, while on a plane from Oakland to Chicago on the way to a DePaul board meeting, I wrote this essay below, knowing that I would someday have a platform to share what it meant to me to be a "Son of DePaul."

Son of DePaul

What does it mean to be a son of DePaul?
As a child of a working-class family, you are drawn to a school where you immediately feel that you belong, and you are claimed as a son of DePaul.
It becomes the first place where you are valued as a person of potential by others outside of your race.
You are given second, third and fourth chances to grow up and realize your potential, because you are a son of DePaul.
You still remember the five philosophy courses that you were required to take as a son of DePaul.
You always have part-time and summer jobs, because in Chicago there is always work for sons of DePaul.
You are 60 years old before you realize, as a Trustee of DePaul, that you were part of a decades-old Vincentian mission and that you were a mission kid.
Many of your most important and oldest friendships are the sons and daughters of DePaul.
De Paul is where you meet your wife of 50 years, a daughter from DePaul and Double Demon (two degrees) of DePaul.
You go to graduate school because your classmates, including your wife, are going to graduate school, and they expect more of themselves and they expect more of you.
You work harder in your chosen field, because you see your classmates becoming successful and you do not want to be an outlier.
You carry a special confidence into the business world, because you are a Double Demon.
Your destiny is to gravitate to a major financial institution, where many of the senior executives graduated from

*Catholic institutions and have a special respect for others
with similar pedigrees.
Even though you are a Baptist, you send your kids to
Catholic schools and volunteer on Catholic boards, because
you highly respect the combination of education and values
that are taught.
You are not allowed to forget that you are a son of DePaul,
and DePaul continually reaches out and reclaims sons of
DePaul.*

Robert (Bob) Steele

At DePaul, I met Bob Steele, the person who would become my
best friend. After undergrad, Bob went to law school at DePaul, and
I went to grad school. On Friday and Saturday nights, Bob and I
would try to find girls at places where guys try to find girls. Bob had
the ability to make girls laugh, which was a high-level skill set when
you are in college. In our pursuit of the fairer sex, we occasionally
ventured into areas in Chicago that were dangerous. On more than
one occasion, we saw the business end of a gun pointed in our
direction.

One of our first jobs after undergrad was working for a local
medium-sized bank in their management training program. One
evening, after working late on a presentation for the next day, we
were part of a part of Chicago life that is all too common.

It was almost midnight, and we were waiting for the next "L"
train, Chicago's famous "elevated" commuter trains, to take us
home. Suddenly, we heard gunshots. Scanning down from our
wooden platform below us, we saw a gunfight. A train approached
while bullets were flying, and people frantically jostled for position
to be first to board.

We made it to safety, but instead of dwelling on the emergency,
Bob and I simply shrugged off the incident (along with other similar
encounters) as being part of the normal rhythm of our lives in
Chicago.

Bob became a successful corporate attorney and retired from
Oscar Meyer in Madison, Wisconsin. If one is fortunate, you have

one great friend in your life. Bob was that friend. Bob transitioned in 2017, and I miss him.

Chapter 4: Jane Aleece Armstrong

"Make no small plans, for they have no power to stir the soul."
~Nicolo Machiavelli

I met Jane Aleece Armstrong in January 1965. As I mentioned earlier, in those days, Chicago public schools had mid-year graduations, and I was one semester behind Jane. I was interested in this quiet, diminutive, and determined woman from the beginning. I was lucky enough and stayed close enough that, by our junior year at DePaul, she agreed that we would live our lives together and get married when we graduated.

In affairs of the heart, traditional wisdom reveals that women *pick* men and then convince men that the men did the picking. One Saturday night, during our early years at DePaul, Jane and I were at a basement party on the south side of Chicago. During a slow dance, she kissed me. At that moment, I knew I had been *picked*. I did not care who did the picking, as long as the result was that we were going to be together.

I married Jane during my senior year. Jane had graduated ahead of me, and she had started a graduate program in Sociology. Jane is another reason why I am a banker today. I was not focused on going to grad school or getting a Master of Business Administration degree until I saw her decide to pursue a master's degree.

To continue our education after getting married, we took out our first loans, two $1,000 National Defense Loans. We were very worried about borrowing money, not realizing how favorable the terms were. The interest rate was three percent, you did not begin paying the loan back until seven years after you graduated, and then you only made quarterly payments until the loan was repaid. The terms were so favorable, we looked forward to making our loan payments.

Jane's family had history with DePaul and teaching was a family business. Her mother had a master's degree in history from DePaul and her sister, Frances, graduated from DePaul's School of Music. Jane, her mother, and Frances all became Chicago public school teachers. Jane primarily taught third grade for 35 years and her mother taught high school history for decades.

Jane was born on April 17, 1947, the eldest sibling of three children. She was soft-spoken, quiet and the most organized person on the planet. Everyone loved Jane because she was as accepting as a person could be, and she was a great listener. Jane had numerous grammar school and high school friends with whom she remained close for all her life.

As an adult, Jane was always available to join community organizations that helped those in need. She was a worker who never sought the spotlight. That made her very popular. One example of Jane's civic works involved Northern Light School in Oakland. It was heavily funded by wealthy Californians and catered to working and middle-class families in Oakland who wanted a private school education for their children at an affordable cost. Jane was a board member at Northern Light for ten years. For most of those years, she quietly served as the board secretary.

Other women loved Jane, and all wanted to befriend her. She was nonjudgmental and discreet. Women knew that they could tell Jane their secrets, fears and frustrations as she listened, empathized, and did not betray their confidences.

One special friend of Jane's was Sharon Deavens. We met Sharon when we moved to Park Forest, Illinois, in 1971. Their friendship survived our move to the west coast and Sharon's frequent moves, primarily to the east coast, for increasing responsibilities for pharmaceutical executive positions.

When Jane was alive, we took numerous vacations together. What was and remains unique about Sharon is that I also regard Sharon as one of my closest friends. I also have a 30-plus year very close friendship with her two sons, Ronald and Jerold, who are now in their 50s. Both are enjoying successful careers. Jerold is the President of a transportation services company that focuses on corporate needs at major sporting events, and Ronald is the Vice Principal of a large suburban high school.

Jane's siblings, Franklin and Frances, are twins,. Franklin was born with special needs. Until Jane's death, she and her sister, Frances, were very protective of him. Frances continues to be Franklin's caregiver, along with her husband, Lawrence. I believe that having a special needs family member had a profound effect on Jane, and it was the reason that she majored in Psychology in college.

As a wife and mother, Jane was selfless. She would not buy anything for herself if she thought that money could be better spent on her kids—or even me. She never wanted a new car and insisted that her car would be the car that I was tired of driving.

In our immediate family, her organizational skills were legendary. She operated out of her checkbook and my checkbook, and every bill was always paid on time. My kids still talk about how Jane would sit and balance our checkbooks to the penny. Jane had her own filing system, and she could find the most obscure document if needed on demand.

Childhood trauma helped shape how frugal and organized Jane became. Her father died of a heart attack when he was only 45, with unsigned insurance papers on his desk. She watched as her mother, a housewife, who had earned a BA in Home Economics from Bennet College in North Carolina, go back to school to get a teaching certificate. Her mother taught high school History until she was 75.

Jane was a student at DePaul when her father passed, and money was extremely tight, but her mother managed to keep her in college, and Frances in a catholic high school. Jane became fiercely loyal and protective of her family after her father's death, and compassionate of her brother's special needs, while understanding that the responsibility of being the breadwinner had been so suddenly thrust upon her mother.

Jane graduated from DePaul with a BA in Psychology and an MA in Sociology. She taught primary grades, mostly third grade, for 40 years. She taught long enough to teach the children of some of her early students. She always taught Black and Brown children from working class neighborhoods. As is the lot of many public-school teachers, she never had enough school supplies, and she routinely spent part of her paycheck on needed supplies for her students.

Modeling my parents' directive to me—to *get accepted at a university and send them the bill*, we told our kids to get accepted at their chosen university and give us the bill. We never saved or borrowed money for our children's education, but we paid for two Catholic high school diplomas, two bachelor's degrees, a master's degree, and a law degree—all from Jane's public-school paycheck.

The one area where Jane would spend money was on vacations. Every year, we went somewhere, and wherever we went, we took the kids. In later years, we started taking two major vacations a year and two minor vacations. We also took our grandkids on vacation with us if they were available.

Our most memorable vacations were to China and Australia. We also loved cruises, especially the ones to Panama, Alaska, and to the Mediterranean. We took multiple vacations to Hawaii, Mexico and the Caribbean. When we lived in Chicago, we drove to Statesville, North Carolina, every other year to visit Jane's relatives. Domestically, we traveled to 30 states in the continental USA, visiting most by car.

When we moved to California in 1986, I promised Jane that I would buy her a home in Chicago when we could afford one. In 2000, we bought a second home in downtown Chicago in the South Loop by Soldiers Field. Since Jane was an elementary school teacher, she was able to spend most summers in Chicago, and we spent every Christmas and New Year's Eve there.

Jane's mother had a Christmas Eve party every year from 1970 until her health began to fail in 2017. Jane and I had a New Year's Eve and a New Year's Day party every year at our Chicago home.

I submit that for most of us, we really don't know who we are marrying until we are married. Jane was a better wife than I expected or deserved. I often told Jane that she would have been a great wife during the Great Depression, because if money became tight, she never complained as she automatically cut back on every household expenditure.

Much success in this life comes from being organized. Jane organized my very unorganized life, and I would not have had the success that I experienced if I had not been married to her. This speech to the 100 Black Men of the Bay Area expresses that sentiment.

100 Black Men of the Bay Area "Lifetime Achievement Award"
December 2017 acceptance speech

Thank you for this "Lifetime Achievement Award." It is not lost on me that you have to be a certain age to qualify for this type of award.

Life is hard. You can do a lot of the right things and still not be successful. The Book of Job says that "Man born of woman is of few days and full of trouble." When I think about my life, I think of Mahalia Jackson singing, "My soul looks back and wonders, how I got over."

As I look back on my life, I can point to three reasons why I have gotten this far. First, over a lifetime, you make thousands of decisions. Some are a lot more important than others. My decision almost fifty years ago to ask Jane Aleece Armstrong to be my bride was the most important decision of my life. Besides being the woman, I loved and my best friend, she came in and organized a very disorganized life.

It has been said that behind every successful executive is a very surprised wife. No one has been more surprised than Jane. She allowed me to live a life where I made no small plans no matter the risk.

It has also been said that you want to live life on the edge, not the center, because you can see things from the edge that you can't see from the center. Jane has supported me living my business life on the edge. Unfortunately, she is battling an illness and could not be here tonight.

The second reason that I am here tonight is that I am blessed with great friends. My friends are the kind of folks that if you are ever in a knife fight, you want these people with you. These are folks that know some of your secrets and they are still your friends. Some of my oldest friends that are here tonight are:

Mike and Denise Lenoir
Al and Maxine Reynolds
Bob and Glenda Harris
Vernon Goins
John Burris
Ces Butner
Rev. Dr. Charlie Hames

*If you want to have a rich life, you can't just hang with old friends.
You must make new friends along the way. Some of my new friends
that are here tonight are:*

Hillard Terry
Biff and Yvette Clark

*Many people in this group tended to know about problems in my
life before I knew that I had problems.*
*The third reason that I am here tonight is because of what the
"100" represents. You want to associate with a group of people
that cheer your success but also let you know if they think that you
are "wandering off the ranch".*
*I do not know of another organization that has a creed like the
"100."*
*No member will be without food for himself or his family, without
clothing, shelter, transportation, legal representation, protection
from violence, or medical care for himself or his family. The last
tenant of the creed is the most important to me, that no member
will ever be without a friend. The creed of the "100" reminds me
of Martin Luther King's famous quote, "Life's most persistent and
urgent question is what are we doing for others?"*
*To every member of the "100," even though I just turned 71, I
believe that the book of my life is still being written and the best
years of my life are ahead of me and as long as I draw breath,
every member of the "100" has a friend in Arnold Grisham.*

The Armstrongs

Jane's parents, Charles Franklin Armstrong and Janice Aleece Knox,
grew up in Statesville, North Carolina. Charles and Janice were high
school sweethearts and had known each other since the third grade.
Jane's father was a valedictorian of John Marshall Law school, night
division. In 1951, he was President of the 6th Ward Democratic
Organization in Chicago and served five terms in the State
Legislature from the 22nd District of Illinois. During his tenure, he
authored the state's gerrymandering statute that became known as
the Armstrong Law (HB113) in 1963. The law promotes integration
in public schools.

Janice and Charles Armstrong
Jane's mother and father

As I mentioned earlier, Charles died suddenly from a heart attack following a bout with pneumonia at age 45, with unsigned insurance contracts on his desk. Janice never remarried and outlived Charles by 50 years, transitioning at age 95.

Cancer

"Between two worlds, life hovers like a star, twixt night and morn, upon the horizon's verge." – Lord Byron

Jane's health was legendary. In fact, I couldn't remember if she or her sister Frances ever had a cold. When we married, Jane weighed 100 pounds, and 45 years later, before she became ill, she weighed 110 pounds. She was the picture of health; that is one reason why her lung cancer diagnosis was so devastating.

A year before she was diagnosed, she developed what appeared to be a severe case of eczema on the palms of her hands. Her doctors treated her for a skin aliment. I mentioned to my doctor, Dr. Rollington Ferguson, that I was planning to take Jane to the Mayo Clinic to see if they could help her with her skin aliment.

Dr. Ferguson asked me if Jane had a cough, and I said, "yes." He knew what the other doctors did not know: that non-small cell lung cancer emits a chemical that causes a reaction on the palms of the hands, resembling eczema. Dr. Ferguson's sharp eye and intellect gave Jane and me more years together because I was able to get her into treatment before her cancer became Stage IV.

Our daughter, Kristine, suspected something was wrong with Jane before the rest of the family. Very little about our family escaped Kristine's gaze. Kristine noticed Jane's cough and reduced energy. I believe that her cancer may have been environmentally caused, because the schools where she taught may have had contaminants and carcinogens.

Jane's first oncologist gave her six months to a year to live because her cancer had already metastasized to both her lungs, but she lived more than five years. Life was difficult, but Jane and I spent most of those five years denying that she had a terminal illness and that there was a date certain (in the near future) that she would die.

During that time, wires from my implanted pacemaker punctured the heart wall, and I passed out on our family room floor. Jane was paralyzed with fear. Kristine, who was there, immediately called 911 and waited in the middle of the street to make sure that the paramedics immediately came to the right house.

We fired the doctor who said that Jane had six months to live. Part of the belief system in the Christian African American Church is that no one this side of creation knows how long any of us will live. In those five years, we were singularly focused on keeping her alive, including two rounds of chemo and two rounds of experimental treatments. Jane never complained.

We took multiple vacations each year and tried to see the world. There were times during her five-year battle that she was very sick, but Jane did not want anyone other than me to know how much she was struggling. There were times in the middle of the night when she would ask me to hold her, and she would say, "I just want to live long enough to see my grandchildren graduate from high school."

There were times when one of my physician friends took me to lunch, and I told him about some new treatment that was being offered that was giving us hope, but the friend would look at me sadly and say, "Arnold, you know this is not going to end well," and I would cry right in front of him.

I was 65 when Jane was diagnosed and 70 when she passed. When Jane transitioned, I was still 65 in my mind because, for the five years that we battled to keep her alive, time stood still.

In Loving Memory
of

Jane Grisham

Apr 17, 1947   January 9, 2018

January 19, 2018

SHILOH CHURCH
Officiating
Pastor George C.L. Cummings

"𝕽emembering…"

The Gospel writer John quotes Christ who said: "Everyone who has life and has committed themselves to me in faith, shall not die for ever."

Today we celebrate Jane Aleece Armstrong Grisham who lived such a life. A devoted wife, mother, grandmother and sister, Jane was a true reflection of God's Grace. Jane was born on April 17, 1947 in Chicago, Illinois, the oldest of three children of Charles and Janice Armstrong. She departed this life on January 9, 2018 at Summit Hospital in Oakland, California.

Jane accepted Christ at an early age at Park Manor Church and graduated near the top of her class at Parker High School both on the South Side of Chicago. She earned a Bachelor of Arts Degree in Psychology and a Masters of Arts Degree in Sociology at DePaul University where she also met her husband, Arnold Terry Grisham.

Jane was a scholar, teacher, mentor and philanthropist. She taught third grade for over 35 years; first at DuBois Grammar School in Chicago and later at Manzanita Grammar School in Oakland. She taught long enough to teach the children of some of her earlier students. Many of her closest friends are the colleagues where she worked in public schools together educating young people from disadvantaged backgrounds.

Jane and Arnold began married life on January 18, 1969. They have two children, daughter Kristine, son Jonathan and three grandchildren Bailey, David and Nola. In 1986 they left the Midwest to take advantage of opportunities in the Bay Area.

Jane and Arnold lived in Oakland for 32 years. In addition to teaching, Jane was an active volunteer and leader in various community philanthropies as well as her church, the Imani Community Church, where she was a trustee for three years.

Jane served for 15 years on the board of trustees of Northern Lights School, a small independent school in Oakland. She was a committed member of Twelve Days of Christmas, a not for profit organization that provides Christmas meals and gifts for children from needy families, and she was a member of Alpha Kappa Alpha Sorority where she actively participated in its charitable endeavors.

Among the activities that she was most proud of is the Last Mile Foundation that she and her husband founded more than ten years ago. It is the fund raising arm of Alive & Free-Omega Boys Club and provides first generation college students with funds to begin their college education. It continues to be very successful granting hundreds of scholarships totaling hundreds of thousands of dollars.

Jane's memory will be cherished by her family; her brother and sister, Franklin and Frances and a host of other relatives and friends. Christ said: "All that the Father gives me, will come to me and those that come to me I will embrace." Jane's legacy is one of taking God's gifts to her and making them available to others. She will be fondly remembered for her big smile, her soft spoken and understanding ways, a quiet yet sharp wit, and her accessible presence that was always available to anyone in need.

Order of Service

PROCESSIONAL

CALL TO WORSHIP   Pastor George C. L. Cummings

SELECTION   Ms. Havis Blanchard
"His Eye is on the Sparrow"

SELECTION   Voices of Faith, Imani Community Church
Mickala Cheadle, Director
"Glory, Honor"

SCRIPTURES

OLD TESTAMENT   Ms. Janice Tounsel
Isaiah 40:28–31

NEW TESTAMENT   Ms. Linda Holliman
1 Corinthians 15:51–54

SELECTION   Ms. Jackie Tolbert
"My Soul is Anchored in The Lord"

EXPRESSIONS (2 MINUTES EACH)

Ms. Kristine Grisham Holliman	Dr. Glenda Newell-Harris
Mr. Jonathan Grisham	Ms. Hellen DeBerry
Ms. Frances Armstrong	Ms. Sharon Deavans
Ms. Tammy Martin	Dr. Michael Lenoir
Ms. Mary Ester Augustine	Ms. Minjon Lenoir

SELECTION   Voices of Faith, Imani Community Church
Mickala Cheadle, Director
"Jesus Will"

ACKNOWLEDGMENTS OF CONDOLENCES   Decature Tounsel

OBITUARY   (Read Silently)

EULOGY   Pastor George C. L. Cummings

SELECTION   Voices of Faith, Imani Community Church
Mickala Cheadle, Director
"Soon and Very Soon"

CLOSING PRAYER

RECESSIONAL

SHILOH CHURCH
3295 SCHOOL STREET
OAKLAND, CA 94602

Honorary Pallbearers

Franklin Armstrong
Mack Bailey
Jonathan Grisham
Lawrence Grisham
David Bryce Holliman
John Martin
Daniel Rucker

Acknowledgment

The family of Jane Grisham wishes to express their
sincere gratitude and appreciation for the many acts of
kindness extended during the loss of their loved one.

Chapter 5: Chicago Banking

"This is the business we've chosen."
~Hyman Roth, The Godfather II

Chicago Banking – The Way Up

My first job after receiving my undergraduate degree from DePaul was working as a supervisor at a Johnson and Johnson manufacturing plant in the Chicago area. At that time, J&J was trying to develop a disposable diaper to compete with Pampers.

My compensation was determined on my working three rotating 8-hour shifts, but I routinely worked 12-hours-on/12-hours-off. I did not mind the extra hours, because Jane and I were saving to buy our first home and J&J paid overtime for the extra hours.

I learned early that Johnson and Johnson was not going to be my life's work. Even though I had a strong math background, I did not have the technical or engineering expertise that many of my peers had. So, I left after one year and went back to DePaul and earned an MBA in Finance.

As I was interviewing with several companies, I had a meeting with a friend who had graduated from DePaul's law school and had become an attorney for a local regional bank in Chicago, Central National Bank. I told him that even with my MBA, I was not certain where I wanted to plant my flag. My friend said, "Consider going into commercial banking. There you will see many industries and companies, and you can then move into your life's work." As it turned out, that meeting changed the course of my life.

At Central National, I learned that banking, especially commercial banking, fit my skill set. I spent one year in a training program where I rotated through various areas of the bank, including writing loan approval summaries for line officers.

After the training period, I spent two years in a commercial banking group that had a portfolio of small Chicago area manufacturers and wholesalers. I loved the work and experiences that I received and even though my friend's counsel was sound, I never wanted to leave banking.

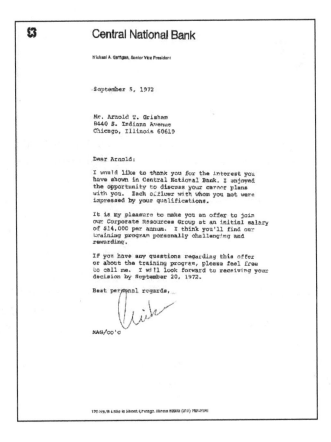

Central National Bank

Michael A. Garrigan, Senior Vice President

September 5, 1972

Mr. Arnold T. Grisham
9440 S. Indiana Avenue
Chicago, Illinois 60619

Dear Arnold:

I would like to thank you for the interest you
have shown in Central National Bank. I enjoyed
the opportunity to discuss your career plans
with you. Each officer with whom you met were
impressed by your qualifications.

It is my pleasure to make you an offer to join
our Corporate Resources Group at an initial salary
of $14,000 per annum. I think you'll find our
training program personally challenging and
rewarding.

If you have any questions regarding this offer
or about the training program, please feel free
to call me. I will look forward to receiving your
decision by September 20, 1972.

Best personal regards,

MAG/co'o

In 1970s Chicago, Continental Illinois National Bank and First Chicago were multinational money center banks and were the two big dogs in Chicago and midwestern banking. I left Central National Bank and was hired by Continental Illinois into a group that banked large companies in the Midwest. My territory was Wisconsin. My customers included SC Johnson, J I Case, Rexnord, Oscar Meyer, Giddings and Lewis, Koller Mfg., the Trane Company and AO Smith.

My routine included traveling to Wisconsin one week each month to meet with customers and prospects. I typically left on Sunday evening and returned on Friday evening, with a considerable amount of time spent on preparing for the trip and following up with requests or issues after the trip.

I spent five years at Continental Illinois, where I enjoyed the business of banking, but I was not on a fast-track. Because Continental was a multinational bank, young bankers with potential were typically offered European assignments. When I asked when I might be considered for an overseas position, my bosses told me that it would be difficult for an African American to be successful in Europe.

They saw me as a journeyman banker who could manage increasingly complex portfolios, but I was not considered to be management material. I knew that if I was going to accomplish my goals, I needed to leave Continental Illinois.

Wells Fargo had a corporate banking office in Chicago, and they wanted to build a business, banking small and medium-sized businesses in the Midwest. Wells Fargo hired me to build a business, banking dealers and distributors of engines and heavy equipment. Eventually, I ran a small business banking group.

Moving to Wells Fargo was a tremendous opportunity and experience. Even though I was 34 years old, Jane and I had never been west of the Mississippi River. In my new position, I was making presentations in San Francisco.

I remember going home one evening and telling Jane that I needed to be careful what I said to my bosses at Wells Fargo, because I felt that they were actually *listening* to me. It was only then that I realized that, at Continental Illinois, I was not being listened to or taken seriously.

Shephard G. Pryor IV was the Regional Manager of our Chicago office. Wells Fargo was a meritocracy, and Shep fit in well. He had no favorites and no agendas, and if you produced, then you were rewarded. His boss, John Lindstedt, was of the same ilk. Because Shep was so bright, he would use allegories, parables or fables to make a point.

At one time, he became worried that San Francisco was getting mixed messages about one aspect of our performance, so he told us the story of the wildebeest. He said that, in Africa wildebeests were safe, as long as they stayed close to the herd, but if they strayed too far from the herd, they could easily be picked off by hungry lions. Everyone clearly got the message and we laughed and retold the story for years.

At the end of my first year at Wells Fargo, we were bringing in a respectable amount of business. I was making $50,000 annually. This was pretty heady compensation for a first line manager in Chicago in 1980. One of our senior managers, Bill Sweet from San Francisco, came to Chicago and presented me with a $5,000 bonus. Jane was incredulous. She said, "They are paying you $50,000, and you get bonuses too?"

I promised Jane that my plan was to establish myself as a commercial banking manager in Chicago, and then find a Chicago opportunity. Our families were in Chicago, so moving to San Francisco would be like moving to Switzerland. The years went by, and I was doing well at Wells Fargo, but it became clear that if I wanted a career at Wells Fargo, I needed to move to San Francisco.

I had a serious job offer from a European bank that would have kept me in Chicago. I would have had three team leaders reporting to me, and I would have overseen the bank's midwestern business. After months of discussion, a senior officer from Europe came to make an offer.

The bank offered me $85,000, plus bonus, housing and car allowance. I accepted their offer, and I went back to my office and called Jane to tell her that we were staying in Chicago. Minutes after I talked to Jane, I got a hurried call from the European Bank.

They said the team leaders who were expected to report to me were rebelling because they felt I was not qualified to be their manager. Even though the bank had given me a firm offer, they said that they never had asked to see a sample of my writing. I told them that our discussions were over and that I was staying with Wells Fargo.

I then called Jane, and I could tell she had tears in her eyes as I told her that we were moving to the San Francisco Bay Area. I wondered if those team leaders would have rebelled if they had been presented with a white manager.

Book Two: Oakland

"Go west, young man." ~*Horace Greeley*

Chapter 6: Oakland and the East Bay

"When you want something, all the universe conspires in helping you to achieve it." ~*Paulo Coelho, The Alchemist*

The Oakland Hills

The topology of the Oakland East Bay hills was different from relatively flat greater Chicago metropolitan area. Many homes had western views, and the sunsets were breathtaking. One very tony area of the Oakland hills was the Montclair District. Many homes were designed with garages at street level, and the residence was built on the side of a hill, beneath the garage. When my real estate agent and I tried to show Jane some of those homes, she would not even get out of the car, because that kind of living was "a bridge too far" for her.

We found a home south of Montclair in the East Oakland Hills, where the homes were on relatively flat land but had great views. We had a view from the San Mateo Bridge to Candlestick Park. Even though I was 39 years old, I had never seen a sunset move across the western sky during different months of the year, because when you live in a urban environment with large buildings, the sun just disappears before it sets.

We paid $213,500 for our Eichler home in 1987, and I sold it for $1,590,000 in 2019.

Holy Names High School and Bishop O'Dowd High School

Even though we were strong public-school advocates in the Chicago area, we enrolled both of our children in private schools in Oakland. Kristine went to Holy Names High School, a famous all girls' Catholic high school. We had heard that girls who go to all girls' schools develop stronger girl friendships than girls who go to co-ed schools. At the writing of this book, Kristine is 52, and she has the same strong girl friendships from Holy Names, and those friendships have endured and grown over the years. She and her friends continue to cheer each other's individual successes and have supported each other during life's inevitable challenges. They are:

Minjon Lenoir-Hall
Casie Johnson
Nicole Ennix
Cherisse Payne
Taja Jacks
Malaika Bobino (later became a member of the group)

Kristine subsequently received her BA in Political Science from University of California at Santa Barbara and her MA in Public Administration from University of San Francisco.

We enrolled our son, Jonathan, in an expensive Episcopalian school in Oakland. It was not a good fit for him or us. I joined the school's board, and my first retreat was at a monastery, where for three days we ate only tofu. Being from the Midwest, I could barely spell tofu. I thought that I was going to starve to death. We eventually moved Jonathan to a Catholic grammar school, where he excelled and was president of his of his eighth-grade class. He was accepted, attended and graduated from Bishop O'Dowd High School in Oakland.

Jonathan went on to become a "Morehouse Man," receiving his BA in Psychology from Morehouse College in Atlanta, Georgia, and he later earned his law degree from Golden Gate University in San Francisco.

"You fit the description of two black men in a black truck who robbed a liquor store in Vallejo."

While generally more progressive and liberal than most of the rest of the country, California has its own familiar racial blind spots. My son, Jonathan (9 at the time) and I played golf one day at the tony Silverado Country Club in Napa, California. At the time, I was driving a new black Jeep Cherokee. As we passed through Vallejo and crossed over the Carquinez Bridge to the East Bay, I noticed that a California State Trooper appeared to be following us.

As I slowed my speed, he slowed his speed and continued to follow us. I felt that the cars around us seemed to know that we were being tailed. As we approached Gilman, a street in Berkeley, the state trooper turned on his light and ordered us to exit the freeway. As we stopped under the Gilman underpass, the white trooper asked us to raise our hands so he could see them. He then asked us to slowly exit the vehicle.

We exited the car with our hands raised high as a small crowd assembled and began to watch. When the trooper saw that we were dressed in golf attire, he said, "You fit the description of two Black men in a black truck who robbed a liquor store in Vallejo.

He stared at us for a moment and then returned to his cruiser and sped away. If we had made a wrong move, the story could have had a different ending. I do remember that he did not apologize for the traumatizing experience. Jonathan, decades later, still reminds me of this event as if it were yesterday.

Today, some might call what happened to us a micro-aggression. Many African Americans call it racially motivated terror. There is a cumulative effect from repeated terror attacks. There is ample research to show that these explicit and implicit terror attacks on Blacks have adversely affected our mental and physical health. Many medical studies suggest it is a primary reason why Blacks have more hypertension than whites.

Kristine Grisham and Grisham Group Executive Search

There are some people in this world who have a natural inclination to study those around them, Kristine is one of those people, and she does not miss much. Despite all of her degrees, we have told her many times that her true calling would have been working for the FBI, or some related entity that would take advantage of her unique insights into people and the human condition.

As I mentioned earlier, Kristine was the first person to notice that Jane's cough was not normal, and she sounded the alarm before the rest of us were suspicious. Similarly, Kristine quickly noticed that something was seriously wrong with me after I passed out on our family room floor after returning home from a routine pacemaker procedure.

She immediately called an ambulance, stood in the middle of the street and directed the emergency technicians to our home. The pacemaker procedure had punctured a hole in my heart wall, so my heart cavity was filling up with blood. If Kristine had not reacted quickly, I would not be here to tell this story.

As a banker loaning money to family businesses, I noticed that in a family business, daughters and fathers tend to work well together. Ego typically does not come into play with fathers and daughters, and daughters tend to focus on the organization's plan and how can the company best make money. When we started our executive search business, I found the search contracts, and Kristine found the candidates.

Years ago, I jotted down the following bullet points that I thought caught the essence of Kristine and some are reflected in my above narrative:

- Kristine is an extremely generous person. If she has a dollar, you have a dollar.
- Kristine can sense evil when it comes into a room. She is very protective of loved ones if that situation occurs.
- If you are ever in a knife fight or in a dark alley with bad people coming in your direction, you want Kristine by your side, or Jonathan.
- Kristine is a quick study. She gets to the conclusion before others do.
- Kristine is mentally tough. You cannot scare her.
- In most situations, Kristine is the smartest person in the room. She is quicker than 99% of the people that she meets.
- Kristine is a monitor. She monitors all her loved ones constantly to make sure that their health is not failing.
- If threatened, Kristine will shoot first and let God separate the saints from the sinners.
- Kristine is one of the most observant people in the universe. She picks up details that others cannot see.
- Kristine wants to be perceived as a good person and wants that to be her legacy.

Jonathan, Fishing and other assorted animals

"Give a man a fish and you feed him for a day. Teach a man to fish and you feed him for a lifetime." ~Tao Tzu

A family is blessed if a father and son can find an activity where they both share a passion, and when the activity is special to them and no one else in the family is remotely interested in what they share. I became hooked on fishing before Jonathan's birth, and I gave him a fishing pole when he was probably three.

We lived in the south suburbs of Chicago. Nearby, there were lakes full of bluegill and crappie that we would frequent. There is nothing that hooks a young boy on fishing more than catching fish. Where we fished, we caught a lot of fish, but we only kept fish that we were going to take home and eat.

In California, the highlight of our fishing years was buying a 19-foot Bass Tracker with our friend, Wallace Hunter. The boat had a deep hull for stability, and it had a fisherman's highchair in back, which became Jonathan's fishing chair. I bought a Jeep Cherokee just so we would have the appropriate vehicle to tow our boat. We fished in northern California lakes, the famous Delta (between the East Bay of California and Sacramento), and we fished in the Sierras.

We were bait cast fishermen versus fly fishermen, so we frequented bait stores and fishing equipment stores all over northern California. We had the most up-to-date fishing gear, including poles and tackle, that money could buy.

We became so obsessed with fishing that we became campers so we could be closer to our fishing destinations. Burney Falls and Lassen Volcanic National Park were our favorite camping and fishing destinations. Since we became campers, we began to take camping-only trips, and our favorite camping destination was Pfeiffer Big Sur State Park.

For two years in early June, when the bears were not quite awake from their winter hibernation, Jonathan and I, along with two of our Oakland friends, Wallace Hunter and John Halley, joined a group from Chicago on a Canadian fishing trip. We met the Chicago contingent in Minneapolis, then flew to Winnipeg, Manitoba, and from there, we took a Canadian flight to Lynn Lake in northern Manitoba.

We then took a float plane to Laurie Lake, further north in Manitoba. The plane landed in a shallow cove in front of our cabin. We brought supplies we needed for a one-week fishing trip, including tackle, food and cooking supplies. We slept in a cabin on the property, and we had two indigenous guides who camped near us.

The fish we were most interested in catching were two-to-three-pound walleye, the largest member of the perch family and a great tasting fish that is plentiful in Canada. Our second favorites were the five-pound lake trout, which were also plentiful. After a successful day, we docked at a deserted island, cooked and ate our catch.

One highlight of the trip was seeing "northern lights" late at night. Wildlife was plentiful, including a pair of bald eagles that had a stone nest in the middle of our lake.

Our trips were not without danger. Late one afternoon, as we were returning from fishing in an adjacent lake, a lightning storm appeared out of nowhere. We were in metal boats and our poles were made of graphite. Jonathan and I were in the last boat to make it back to shore, when our motor failed.

Our friend John Halley saw our predicament, and along with two other Chicago friends, John Peck and Byron LeGardy, came back to our location and rescued us by towing us back to shore. Towing us back significantly increased their chances of being hit by lightning, because towing the two boats meant that both boats were in the water 45 minutes longer than they should have been—in the middle of a lightning storm. We all remember Jonathan asking me if we were going to die, and I recall not having a reassuring answer for him.

Jonathan, for all his life, has been interested in animals and has had a deep academic understanding of the animal kingdom. Even though he is a Morehouse College graduate and a Golden Gate University law school graduate, his real calling is probably in some form of animal science.

Growing up, Jonathan has had a variety of cats, dogs, turtles, fish and other assorted animals as pets. One evening, as Jane's car pulled into our garage, I could hear her screaming at Jonathan. She had taken him to a pet store to buy some form of rodent. Jonathan had opened the cage while Jane was driving, and the animal escaped and apparently ran across Jane's feet. It was the only time I heard her raise her voice at one of the kids, as she thought that she was going to have a heart attack.

Because Jonathan loved animals, we became "zoo" people, and every trip we took, we tried to visit the local zoo. Our favorite trip was to the Sidney Zoo in Australia. Our US favorite was the San Diego Zoo.

During our Australia trip, we flew from Sidney to Cains to snorkel the Great Barrier Reef. It was the trip of a lifetime to see the variety and size of fish that passed in front of us. After our snorkel, we took a helicopter ride over the reef, where we saw 20-foot sharks. If we had taken the helicopter ride first, we would have never put a toe in the water.

Father and Son Fishing Trips

Bailey, David and Nola — Grandkids

Carla Glasser theorized that parents take too much credit when their children are successful and too much blame when they are not. Bailey, age 19, is a great example. She was focused and eggy coming out of the womb. Her quote in my epilogue is an example of her focus.

She combines mother wit and hard work to be successful in any environment. She willed her way into UCLA, and she frequently tells me, "Grandpa, do not worry about me. I am fine."

David is our athlete, and he is one of the smartest in our family. At 18 and 6'4," he has an excellent breaststroke and back-stroke. He also has the "golden arm" and will pitch for his high school with a 94-mph fastball next season. In track and field, he anchors his school's 4x100-meter track relay team that could compete for state honors. He also is a contender in the 200-meter hurdles.

Nola, age 12 (also very smart), is the sweetest, nicest and kindest person in our family. It is a joy to watch her grow.

Serendipity Books

The Oakland that my family experienced for 30 years, beginning in 1987, was a very special place. There was an eclectic and funky feel to the city. From restaurants to bookstores to small boutiques and art galleries, there was an academic and beatnik vibe to the city that is hard to describe.

There were days when I could walk down Grand, Telegraph, or College Avenues and just be entertained by all that came within my view. I saw and became enthralled by bookstores that had rare books—so fascinated that I became a rare book collector. Many of the 1,000 first editions and other rare books that I found and bought came from local East Bay Area bookstores.

My favorite bookstore was Serendipity Books in Berkeley, where the owner specialized in various genres, including African American rare books. The owner, Peter Howard, was a legendary antiquarian bookseller who had amassed over one million books at the time of his death from pancreatic cancer in 2011.

Sequoyah Country Club

In the 1980's, when an employee reached a certain level at Wells Fargo, especially in a position dealing directly with customers, the executive could join a country club and the bank would pay for the membership. Many of my customers belonged to country clubs.

There are two clubs in Oakland – Claremont Country Club and Sequoyah Country Club. During the 1980s, I thought the Claremont Country Club had the feel of an old-line generational club, where the initiation process appeared to be very formal and appeared to include getting to know one's wife.

The wife part would have been a problem for me, because when we lived in the Chicago area, most country clubs appeared to discriminate against African Americans. We lived in a community where we felt hostility and discrimination from the local country club. So, Jane was not feeling it when I told her that the bank was paying me to join a country club. Adding fuel to the fire, Wells Fargo gave me $30,000 to join Sequoyah Country Club while Jane was spending part of her paycheck to buy pencils for her students.

From a membership standpoint, Sequoyah had the feel of "first generation entrepreneurs who had made their own money," whereas Claremont to me had the feel of second or third generational wealth. Jane gave me the go ahead to join Sequoyah, as long as I did not tell any of her friends.

Marcus Foster Educational Institute, Dr Coyness Ennix, MD and Ada Cole

I was on the board of numerous not-for-profit organizations in Oakland, but my favorite was the Marcus Foster Educational Institute. Marcus Foster was a superintendent of the Oakland Unified School District from 1970 to 1973, when he was assassinated by the Symbionese Liberation Army (SLA).

The urban terrorist group said it murdered Foster for allegedly supporting of a plan to require a student identification card in the

Oakland school system—an action they called "fascist." The proposed program was intended to reduce vagrancy and keep non-student drug-dealers off the districts' campuses, and Foster had already gained support from the school board to modify the program to meet community concerns.

While he was superintendent, Foster founded the Oakland Education Institute to raise money to fund projects that could not be funded through normal educational channels. After his death, the institute was renamed the Marcus Foster Educational Institute. I have fond memories of the Institute, not only because I believed in its work, but because of the extraordinary people I met who were also associated with the Institute.

Ada Cole, the Executive Director, recruited me to the Institute's board. She had an understated, powerful presence, especially when it came to fundraising. I was able to secure annual contributions to the Institute from Wells Fargo Bank's foundation.

Once, shortly after getting the bank's foundation to write a check, Ada called me and said, "Arnold, we need an additional grant." I answered, "Your request is coming too soon after the grant that we just provided." Following a momentary silence, Ada insisted, "Arnold, you can *do* this!"

With that brief statement, I understood that it would be easier for me to convince Wells Fargo's foundation to write another check than it would be to tell Ada Cole that I could not get it done. I had not met anyone in the not-for-profit world who had Ada's presence and personal power when it came to fundraising—nor have I not met anyone since.

Dr. Coyness L. Ennix Jr., one of my close friends, was also on the Board. Ennix was one of the few surgeons in the world who perfected the technique of operating on a beating heart. If the heart is not stopped during surgery, the patient's recovery time is shorter.

He was a young resident at Highland Hospital in Oakland when Marcus Foster and his deputy, Robert Blackburn, were brought to the hospital, after being shot numerous times. Foster died as he was purposely and senselessly shot in the head by one of the assailants.

Blackburn survived 20 bullet wounds from a sawed-off shotgun. A team of physicians, led by Dr. Ennix, worked all night – with Blackburn's heart stopping twice – and saved Blackburn's life. Dr.

Ennix has been tied to Marcus Foster and the Institute ever since, and he was recently named chairman of the Institute's Board.

"Angels on Horseback," "Big Thinkers" and "Truth Tellers" in Oakland and the East Bay

For people who grow up in larger cities, like Chicago, relationships tend to be limited to professional silos. Yet for those in medium-sized communities like Oakland, they naturally meet and get to know people in disciplines that are very different from those in their personal silos. During my time in Oakland, here is a list of some of the people who have enriched my life and have caused me to see a bigger world than I knew existed.

Barry Williams and Lalita Tademy

Barry was the first person I met when I moved to Oakland. We had a mutual friend, Peter Bynoe, who was a prominent Chicagoan, and like Barry, a Harvard alum. Barry had three degrees from Harvard (a BA, an MBA and a JD), and he captained Harvard's basketball team. When I met Barry, he was also a board member on Harvard University's Board of Overseers.

Barry embraced me, from virtually the initial day I came to Oakland in 1986, and he hosted a dinner for me to meet other up-and-coming Oaklanders at a trendy restaurant on Grand Avenue in Oakland. I will never forget that the first thing I saw on the menu was an oyster appetizer called "Angels on Horseback." At that moment, I realized that I had "burned the boat!" I would not be going back to Chicago.

Barry was responsible for introducing my family to St Paul's School, an Episcopalian grammar school in Oakland, where Jonathan enrolled as a third grader. I joined the board and soon thereafter attended a spiritual avant-garde board retreat in Marin, California, where we only ate tofu for three days.

Being a Chicagoan, I could barely spell tofu. After three days of eating only tofu, I thought I was going to starve to death—another reminder that I was no longer in Chicago.

My association with Barry caused me to step up my game, and I began to have aspirations that I never had in Chicago. During the 1980s, Barry was the most senior Black executive west of the Mississippi river, and he was in constant demand by large corporations to join their board of directors.

When I asked Barry how I could make myself attractive as a prospective board member, his answer was that I should prepare myself to be an audit chair. He said that no one wanted to be a board audit chair because of the amount of work required. With that knowledge, my first board opportunity was with a young company that was looking specifically for an audit chair.

As an aside, while working with Carl Reichardt, the then-Chairman of Wells Fargo, I became close enough to him chairing the bank's first cultural diversity committee that I was able ask him the same question: How can I make myself an attractive corporate board candidate?

His response to me was, "When are you going to join the Party?" and he was not talking about the Democratic party. I did not join the Republican Party, and we never discussed the subject again. Carl had no way of knowing that I came from a family of Democrats. Since then, I have wondered how many African Americans have been recruited or co-opted into the Republican Party in a similar fashion.

Barry's wife, Lalita Tademy, is the author of *Cane River*, an Oprah Winfrey Book Club and *New York Times* bestseller. She is also the author of *Red River* and *Citizens' Creek*. Lalita has been an inspiration to all of us would-be writers.

I have been very fortunate, because Barry and Lilita's world continues to expose my family to new avant-garde cultural content and likeminded people.

Michael Lenoir, MD and Denise Lenoir, MSN

Mike Lenoir is a true Renaissance man. As a physician, Mike has a number of specialties, including internal medicine, pediatrics and allergy and immunology. When I met Mike, he had a private medical practice, a radio show, a TV show and a daily "medical minute" radio segment, where he would discuss relevant medical topics. Mike has had one of the largest medical practices in Northern California, and he has been the Doc for all of my friends' kids over the years Mike has formed many organizations to eliminate the disparities in healthcare for African Americans, including The Ethnic Health Institute and the African American Wellness Project.

Mike and I met because our daughters became close friends at Holy Names High School in Oakland. Mike is a past president of the National Medical Association. When I met Mike, he was also a reserve US Army Lieutenant Colonel in the Army Medical Corps, and at that time, he had the distinction of being the youngest commissioned Lieutenant Colonel in the U.S. Army Medical Corps.

Mike is one of the smartest people I know. He has the rare combination of having a photographic memory and a very quick mind. Mike is a content creator, and most of the content Mike creates consists of unedited first-take compositions. Sometimes, after a round of golf in a clubhouse, Mike will describe every shot he made over 18 holes, and then he will describe every shot I made.

Everyone needs at least one person in their life who is brutally honest with them about their failings. Mike is that person in my life. On the golf course: "Arnold, a good golfer would never do what you just did," "Arnold, what were you thinking?" On health: "Arnold, you need to lose weight." I answered "Mike, I don't think that I have gained much weight!" His response: "Arnold, when you look in the mirror, turn to the side".

Denise, Mike's wife, was an RN and a FNP (Nurse Practitioner) and she and Mike practice together. There is a saying: It takes a village to raise a child. That only works if the village has Denise Lenoirs in the village. There are some people who are more observant than the rest of us. Denise is one of the most nonjudgmental people I know. She does not miss much and has consistently known more about my kids than I have.

In the past ten years, I have had two major health-related events. First, I was struck by a car and ended up in the emergency room at Highland Hospital in Oakland. The second health event as I mentioned earlier occurred when I was being transported to the emergency room at Sutter Medical Center in Oakland because my heart wall was pierced in a routine pacemaker surgery.

During both occurrences, when I looked up from my hospital bed, Mike and Denise were there, making sure that I had "people," and the medical staff knew I had "people" who cared about me.

Robert Harris and Glenda Newel Harris, MD

Bob and Glenda are an extraordinary couple in my world. Both have led a number of national African American fraternal and professional organizations, including The National Bar Association, Kappa Alpha Psi Fraternity, Sigma Pi Phi Fraternity and The Links Incorporated. They both live their lives promoting the health, well-being and the advancement of African Americans.

They both are published authors, Bob, with *Goodbye Arkadelphia!. Turning Obstacles into Opportunities.* Bob's book is his life history in memoir form, and each chapter is a self-contained segment of his life. Glenda's book, written with Brenda Spriggs, is a primer on taking charge of your health, titled, *Focus on Your Best Health, Smart Guide to the Health Care You Deserve.*

Everyone in this section of my book has benefited community organizations and has mentored those that have followed them. Bob has done more than anyone that I know to benefit individuals and organizations with his time and financial resources. He tirelessly works to help others, especially African Americans. When I am with Bob, I realize I need to do more.

Both have received numerous awards and accolades, and each has been honored by their respective academic institutions, with Glenda recently having The Glenda Newell-Harris' 71 Student Center named in her honor.

This book is a direct result of me paying attention to how Bob structured his book, with each chapter being its own memoir, as I mentioned above. If I had not seen and embraced Bob's template, I would have never written this book. This is another example of the benefits from hanging around smart "can-do" friends.

Coyness Ennix, MD and Kathy Ennix

Like Mike Lenoir, I met Coyness because our daughters were classmates at Holy Names High School in Oakland. As I mentioned earlier, Coyness had early notoriety, because he was the attending resident at Highland Hospital in Oakland when Marcus Foster and his deputy school superintendent were brought to Highland Hospital after being attacked by the Symbionese Liberation Army.

As Paulina and I began to learn about each other's friends, I discovered the high regard that the staff at Merritt Hospital, the predecessor of Alta Bates Summit Medical Center in Oakland, had of Dr Coyness Ennix.

Paulina was the Nurse Executive at Merritt Hospital during Coyness' prime practicing years at the hospital. She said that when Coyness walked into the hospital, she would get a note that "Dr Ennix is in the building." He was so respected that, when waiting for an elevator, any crowd also waitng for the elevator would part so that Dr Ennix could enter first.

Coyness once told me that his mother took him to see a specialist when he was a young boy. After spending a short period of time with them, the doctor charged his mother a few hundred dollars.

His mother asked the doctor, "Why am I being charged so much, when you did not spend much time with us?" The doctor responded, "Ma'am, you are paying me for what I know—not for what I do."

As they left the doctor's office Coyness' mother said to her son, "I want you to become a specialist." Thus, the inspirational birth of a Thoracic Surgeon!

As I said earlier, it takes a village to raise a child. Cathy Ennix, like Denise Lenoir, was part of the village that helped to raise all our children.

James Cole and Ada Cole

Jim and Ada were the second couple who I met when I moved to Oakland. They had met when they were students at Talladega College in Talladega, Alabama. Ada's surname was also Cole, so it was not clear if she kept her maiden name when they married or whether she took his name. Jim, a graduate of Harvard Law School, was also a past president of The National Bar Association and a past president of Sigma Pi Phi Fraternity, the oldest African American Greek letter fraternity in America, founded in 1904, and he was my sponsor into the fraternity.

Ada, from a distance, adopted our daughter, Kristine and continues to be a close family friend. She brought me into The Marcus Foster Institute in Oakland as a board member and caused me to become a subsequent Chairman of Marcus Foster's board. Ada and Marcus Foster are discussed earlier in this chapter.

George Strait

One can measure one's net worth in financial terms, or one can choose to measure net worth in terms of the richness of friendships. George is an example of my having tremendous equity in the richness of my friendships. In Chicago, I never knew or had the opportunity to have a friend like George Strait, who was far removed from my professional silo. George instinctively monitored friends from a distance and offered to be of service when he saw his skills were needed.

George is a senior communications executive, and he has held senior executive positions at the FDA, The National Institutes of Health and the University of California, Berkeley. Additionally, George had a 22-year career at ABC News, where he was Chief Medical Correspondent and White House Correspondent, among other important positions.

In watching my family deal with the death of Jane from a distance, George found the appropriate time to ask if he could edit the obituary that I had written. His editing, with the religious vignettes, turned the program appearing in the Jane Grisham section into a keepsake for our friends and family.

George is the editor of this book, and he is responsible for the title, *Making a Way Out of No Way: An African American Journey*. He is also responsible for pushing me to write an epitaph. George said, "When someone reads your book, what is the takeaway that you want to leave with them?" Because of George's push, the epitaph is an important part of this book.

Vernon Goins

Vernon is Paulina's and my attorney, and I believe he has grown one of the most successful law firms in Alameda County. In this collection of unique individuals, Vernon is the youngest, at age 54. He was born in Berkeley to a mother who was a "progressive" before the term was popularized. She enrolled him in the French American International School in San Francisco and sent him to a boarding school in Paris for high school.

There, he met the children of many of the leaders in French-speaking West Africa. Vernon is one of the most educated people I know. Besides English, Vernon is fluent in French and Spanish. He has four degrees: a BA from Georgetown University, an MBA from The University of Laverne in Southern California, a Juris Doctorate from the University of California, College of the Law, and a LLM in Taxation from Golden Gate University in San Francisco.

Vernon introduced me to Paulina and was responsible for our first date, a blind date. We were and continue to be clients and friends of his.

During the pandemic, Vernon taught me to be gentle with people who might approach any of us in a sideways (or less than friendly) manner. He said, "This period has been so traumatic for families. You do not know what that person who is coming in your direction has been through, and you do not know the stress level of the last three conversations that person may have had before they talked to you".

Vernon is one of the most selfless people I know, giving significant time and money to various causes. He is also the prototype of the "trusted advisor." His photographic memory has contributed to part of his success, along with his ability to simplify complexity.

Not only does he know most of my family's secrets, but he also probably knows some of our secrets that we do not consciously *know* are secrets.

Maxine Reynolds

Maxine and Al Reynolds were a California success story and a California love story. They married in South Carolina, when she was 19 and he was in his 20s. They moved to Detroit, where Al learned the property management business and subsequently brought those skills to Northern California. If Maxine wanted or needed anything, Al would find a way to provide it.

While Al was building his business in the Bay Area, Maxine was a Wells Fargo branch manager. Some of the toughest women in America have been Wells Fargo branch managers. Maxine's branch was called "University Ave Branch." It was in a "sketchy" part of Berkeley and was frequently robbed.

Wells Fargo branch managers were known for their toughness and were difficult to scare. One branch manager became famous when she slipped a note back to a would-be robber, demanding money: she told him that he had to get to the end of the line, just like everyone else. When he complied, the police were called to take the not-too-bright robber to jail.

Maxine was the prototype first line "public facing" supervisor. She had seen it all, and nothing could scare her. In an alley, with bad guys coming in your direction, anyone would want Maxine with them. Occasionally, Maxine and I would be engaged in a kerfuffle with one of our constituents, and Maxine would tell me that she could hurt that individual in more colorful language than I could describe in this passage. I did not realize until she had a foot injury and could not wear her signature high heel shoes that her presence belied her true height.

Even though Maxine and I were Wells Fargo alumni, we met when we started Alta Alliance Bank in Oakland. At Alta Alliance, she was a relationship manager, handling the deposit and borrowing needs of customers. Many in Oakland wanted Maxine to handle their banking needs. Years later, Maxine moved with me to Tri-Valley Bank, where she continued to be the banker of choice in the East Bay.

As I wrote this book, Maxine had lost her beloved, Al, after their 58-year marriage and was preparing for the next stage of her life.

Walter Johnson

When I met Walter, he was Director of Retirement Systems and later Director of Personnel for the City of Oakland. Our sons attended a small catholic school in the Oakland Hills together that I mentioned earlier. We became close friends when we led a parent's group to provide extra scholastic materials that the school could not afford.

Walter is one of the most nonjudgmental people I know. People could tell Walter their darkest secrets, knowing Walter could be trusted. When people have "stuff" where they need a helping hand, the first person they would call was Walter. Walter is also a devout Christian, so when I call Walter for advice, I know that his advice is Christian based.

Decature Tounsel

All my Oakland friends are African Americans, and they have had a long relationship with me and my family. Yet there is one more, Decature Tounsel. Decature is a Chicagoan who I have known for approximately 50 years. He, too, is a great friend and has had a deep impact on my family. We met when I was a junior banker at Continental Illinois National Bank in Chicago and Decature was an Inroads Fellow. Inroads is an organization that prepares students from diverse backgrounds to succeed in the workplace.

Our friendship grew quickly because our journeys were so similar. We were both from the south side of Chicago, children of working-class families, and we were two of the few Blacks in commercial banking in the 1970s.

Decature did not have much financial or emotional support from his family. From an early age, he raised himself and learned to navigate the world virtually on his own. Both of Decature's parents were ill for years and died when he was in his early 20s.

Because of our age difference (I was 27 and Decature was 17) and because I was a Black unicorn in corporate America having some early success—a wife, two kids and a home in the suburbs, I became a role model for Decature. When I had an opportunity to move away from Continental and join Wells Fargo in Chicago, Decature walked over to our offices with his resume and asked if he also could join the bank.

Decature had a successful five-year run at Wells Fargo and was recruited to join Discover Card at an executive level when the company was in its infancy. When Discover Card was bought by Morgan Stanley, Decature enjoyed significant financial gains. Decature's journey is an "Only in America" story, beginning humbly and achieving singular success.

At some point on our collective journeys, and as I have become older, Decature has become a protector of my family. At many family events, Decature has come to California on his own dime and taken a leadership role. With my children, Decature is an unapologetic truth teller. His truth is valued for the perspective he gained from his early life. My family has been blessed to have Decature in our lives.

Chapter 7: Wells Fargo Bank

"I want to stand as close to the edge as I can without going over. Out on the edge you can see all kinds of things you can't see from the center." ~Kurt Vonnegut

Bay Area Commercial Banking – Learning the Way

Middle-market commercial banking in the mid-eighties and early nineties was defined as "banking companies with revenues of under $250 million" or "wealthy individuals with borrowing needs of over $1 million." Midwestern commercial banking was very competitive, and new banking opportunities did not occur frequently for most banks.

Because of Wells Fargo's preeminent position in the marketplace (California being a magnet for new entrepreneurs) and a booming California economy, our Oakland commercial banking office constantly saw new banking opportunities for new customers and new opportunities for existing customers that needed their financings increased or restructured.

My first position in our Oakland commercial banking office was Loan Team Manager. Each commercial banking office had a regional manager, commercial bankers, private bankers, credit department, note department, and a loan approver or loan team manager.

I felt that my credit skills increased dramatically simply because of the volume of deals I saw. I was born for this business, and every day was intoxicating. Lou Cosso was the regional manager of the Oakland Regional Commercial Banking Office when I arrived. He was initially suspicious of a new loan team manager being forced on him by corporate, but like Pryor and Lindstedt, who as I mentioned earlier were my first bosses before him, he ran a meritocracy.

He and I constantly talked and did deals. Sometimes, we would change clothes at 4:00 p.m. and run around Lake Merritt, discussing deals. The jog was 3.2 miles. If we were not finished talking after one lap, Lou would say, "Let's go again," and we would run around the lake a second a second time. Often what followed the run was a meeting with a couple of lenders over a glass of wine, where we continued to talk about credit and deals. Then I would go home, have dinner with the family, sit in front of the TV and do paperwork until I fell asleep. As I have said many times, I never needed an alarm clock to wake up the next day, because my job woke me up.

This was my routine for years as a loan team manager and subsequently as a commercial banking regional manager. I felt that I was one of the blessed people on Earth, because I never felt like I was working. To this day, Lou Cosso is one of my closest friends.

"Run it like you own it." and "Ask for forgiveness, not permission."- Wells Fargo-isms

I was a careful banker, but I knew how to "read the room". Every business in Wells Fargo had its own balance sheet and income statement. We were given a lot of leeway on running our business, but we had to make our numbers.

As a regional commercial banking manager, I had a $5 million credit limit for new deals and a $20 million limit for approving increases to existing customers. I remember calling my boss in San Francisco to discuss a large deal that we were considering, and as I began speaking, he said to me, "Grisham, if I need to help you with this decision, why do I need you?" Click.

In the late 1980s, I was in the midst of trying to book a nine-figure loan. At that time, it would be the largest deal that our commercial banking group had ever booked. I was negotiating with the borrower in his offices (the borrower was from a different culture). Late in the evening, he told me that we could have the loan if I would reduce his rate by 25 basis points. I left his office and called my boss, who was angry with me because the deal was not done, and he breathed fire at me through the phone. With his disappointment evident, he said, "I will call you back."

He had to go to Carl Reichardt, the bank's Chairman and CEO, to get the 25 basis point reduction on a nine-figure loan. He called me back and said, "You have the 25 basis points, but if you don't have a signed deal in your briefcase, don't come back." Fortunately for me, I was able to get the loan document signed and keep my job.

I had another large deal that I was trying to get approved, and one of the bank's vice chairmen heard about it and made it clear that he did not think that we should do it. In response, Charlie Johnson, a vice chairman who was also one of my bosses and head of commercial banking systemwide, called me and asked why I *liked* the deal. When I told him, he said, "Fuck it. Let's do it."

Expense Control – Carl Reichardt and Kim Keenan

Carl E. Reichardt, the former chairman of Wells Fargo, was legendary in his quest for expense control and running lean, efficient businesses. He used an old chair in his office that had stuffing falling out from the sides. If you had the misfortune of having to ask him for more resources for whatever reason, he would start pushing stuffing back into the chair.

Early one year, I had one loan team manager leave and a new manager arrive. The new manager asked our admin, Kim Keenan, to order a new calendar. She responded that the former manager's calendar had barely been used, and that it would be a waste of money to buy a new calendar.

Sometime after that exchange, when I was on a customer call with Charlie Johnson, I told him how Carl's cost-cutting culture was getting through to the troops. The next day, Carl called Kim Kenan and thanked her for looking out for the shareholders of Well Fargo Bank. Kim was so stunned that she could barely speak.

Wells Fargo's First Cultural Diversity Committee

In 1992, Carl Reichardt decided to form the bank's first Cultural Diversity Committee. Many people he respected had told him that CEOs needed to take a leadership role in promoting diversity in their organizations. Carl told me that I would be the first chairman of the committee. I did not shy away from this responsibility, but I had not asked for the new responsibility either. I was to report directly to Carl and to report on the committee's progress in making the bank more diverse.

I typically met with Carl around 6 a.m. to discuss our strategy and progress. During one of our first meetings with Steve Enna, our head of Human Resources, we discussed the tools we could use to make the organization more diverse. We decided to hire a diversity consultant, hold seminars, and make diversity a business issue, because our customer base was diverse. We would count people and drive numbers, like we drove numbers in other initiatives.

I told Carl that as a Black executive I had lived through the white backlash that had resulted from affirmative action initiatives, and there would be a backlash and resentment if our initiative looked like affirmative action.

Carl responded, "Arnold, we could do this your way, but if things get fucked up, I will personally kick your ass." Carl also said, "I do not have time to change how people think, but through fear I can change how they behave. And, over time, if their behavior changes, maybe their minds will change."

Steve Enna was sitting between us, and through the corner of my eye, I saw him back up slightly—just in case Carl wanted to get more personal with me.

We Counted Everybody.

Early on, Carl asked me to meet with all the vice chairmen to discuss how we would roll out the work of the committee. I took Regina Muehlhauser, a senior executive in the bank and committee member, with me to the various meetings. As we were talking to one of the vice chairmen about his organization, he rose and closed the door to his office. Then he said, "It is important for both of you to realize, Carl does not run this bank. We do."

His message was, *Don't get too far over your skis on this initiative.* As we left the vice chairman's office, our unspoken words to each other were, "How are we going to survive this struggle?"

One reason Carl decided to make the bank more diverse was his experience with being on the Ford Motor Company Board, listening to a fellow board member, Clifton R Wharton, Jr. Clifton Wharton was the then-Chairman of The Teachers Insurance and Annuity Association of America-College Retirement Fund.

He shared with Carl his progress in making his company more diverse. Carl asked me to fly to New York to meet with Wharton and tell him about our initiatives and our progress to date, Wharton smiled at me and told me to tell Carl, "While everything we were doing was admirable, there really was only one thing that he needed to do to quickly create a more diverse company."

That one thing was to personally set an example by having diverse executives report to him. Wharton said that executives model their boss's behavior on business issues. For instance, Carl was a cost-cutter, so we all became cost-cutters. Wharton continued, "When Carl has diverse execs reporting to him, his direct reports will find diverse execs to report to them."

When I returned, I delivered Wharton's message to Carl at our next early morning meeting. Carl smiled, and I left. Carl never had a diverse executive running a revenue business report to him before he retired, and I believe that only recently has any Wells Fargo CEO since Carl met Wharton's test. Notwithstanding Wharton's test, Carl Reichardt was ahead of his time.

Executive Vice President

One morning, as I was crossing the Bay Bridge on my way to San Francisco, my boss called me and said, "Grisham, get your butt in my office. The board has just elected you as an Executive Vice President."

I never asked to be an executive vice president. I was still suffering from the imposter syndrome associated with being a senior vice president. I was still the kid whose father had looked at him on his death bed and said, "Boy, you sure are ugly."

I pulled into Embarcadero One in San Francisco and wrapped my car around a post. Adding fuel to the fire, one of my bosses, Hardy Watford, said to me, "The good news is, now you have a bigger gun—the bad news is that there are new people that are going to hate you, and they have big guns, too."

I believe that my promotion to executive vice president was one of Carl Richardt's last official acts before he retired. When Carl left Wells Fargo, I wrote the following letter to him.

WELLS FARGO BANK

ARNOLD T. GRISHAM
Executive Vice President

One Kaiser Center Plaza, Suite 850
Oakland, CA 94612

August 10, 1994

Mr. Carl E. Reichardt
Chairman of the Board &
Chief Executive Officer

Dear Carl,

You have influenced many lives during your career, including
mine. A defining moment for me occurred when you asked me to
chair the Cultural Diversity Committee.

I recently read a passage written by Howard Thurman that
described the experience that you gave me. "...what happens when
a person is pulled out of the regular routine of his life by some
issue and finds himself standing up to be counted. It is a
crucial experience. It means that a person is willing to take
full responsibility for his actions, actions that extend beyond
his little world, actions which may involve him in risk, foreign
both to his temperament and his life plan."

You probably had more confidence in me then than I had in myself
and I will always be grateful for the push that you gave me and
for your continuing support.

For those of us you are leaving behind, it is important for us to
remember that the quality and richness of our lives is enhanced
by our ability to influence other lives in the way that you have
influenced ours.

Although you are retiring as Chairman of Wells Fargo & Co., I am
certain that you are not retiring from being a major positive
influence on as large a stage as you deem appropriate.

Carl, thank you for the opportunities and the experiences.

Best personal regards,

Arnold

Printed on Recycled Paper

SECRETARY'S CERTIFICATE

I, Guy Rounsaville, Jr., Secretary of Wells Fargo Bank, National Association (the "Bank"), a national banking association, do hereby certify that the following is a true and correct copy of a resolution duly adopted by the Board of Directors of the Bank at a meeting duly held on May 17, 1994:

RESOLUTION NO. 94-029: ELECTION OF OFFICER

Following introductory remarks by the Chairman, on motion duly made, seconded and unanimously carried, the following resolution was adopted:

RESOLVED, that the following named individual be, and he hereby is, appointed to the office shown opposite his name:

Arnold T. Grisham   Executive Vice President

I further certify that such resolution appears of record in the minutes of said meeting, in the official minute book of the Bank, and that said resolution is now in full force and effect and has not been modified, rescinded or repealed as of the date of this certificate.

IN WITNESS WHEREOF, I have hereunto affixed my signature and the seal of the Bank on this 16th day of June, 1994.

Guy Rounsaville, Jr.
Secretary

Chapter 8: Entrepreneurship, Community Banking, The Federal Reserve Bank and Tri-Valley Bank

"The problem is we are all surrounded with insurmountable opportunities." ~Pogo

Community Banking and Entrepreneurship

While working at Well Fargo, one of my responsibilities was running the bank's corresponding banking business nationwide. The challenge involved managing the bank's relationship with other U.S. banks. In addition to having an inside view of large banks across the country, I also had an inside view of community banks.

I concluded that community bankers were having more fun and were happier than my peers at the larger banks. They were true entrepreneurs. Their lives were not as complex, they were not getting hundreds of emails every day, they had closer relationships with their customers and their communities, they were viewed more positively than their peers at larger banks, and they had more control over their balance sheets.

I became envious of my community bank colleagues. In 1998, Wells Fargo merged with another big bank, Norwest. The culture was changing, so I seized the opportunity to leave and enter this new world of community banking.

I had two short tenures at Civic Bank of Commerce, a local community bank in Oakland, where I served as president, chief lending officer and chief operating officer. Also I served as a partner in the financial services practice of Korn Ferry, the large executive search firm.

I learned community banking from the inside at Civic Bank of Commerce. My work at Korn Ferry was similar to my corresponding banking experience, both giving me a view of community banking from 30,000 feet, and because in doing C level searches for banks, I continued to educate myself on the various models of community banking.

I was lured away from Civic Bank to Korn Ferry by my daughter, Kristine. She was a recruiter at Korn Ferry at the time. By all accounts, she was the first daughter to recruit her father into a large executive search firm. After learning the executive search business, Kristine and I started our own, the Grisham Group Executive Search.

We specialized in C level community banking searches, not-for-profit searches and large company diversity searches. I found the new searches for our firm, and Kristine found the candidates. We developed a good customer base of repeat business and had a successful run for five years.

After I left the search business, Kristine decided to go in-house and became a "go-to" search professional for Bay Area start-ups.

Kristine recently accepted a position with Sony Electronics in San Diego as Head of Diversity and Talent Acquisition.

Alta Alliance Bank

While we were doing C level searches for community banks, I began to see some of my peers starting new (de novo) banks. I told Kristine that I was going to leave the search business and start a bank. So, in 2007, with a group of investors and Western Alliance Bank, a large Las Vegas Bank, we started Alta Alliance Bank, which became a wholly owned subsidiary of Western Alliance.

Our timing was terrible. The Great Recession began later that year and lasted until the beginning of 2011. Western Alliance Bank was a well-run bank, but all banks struggled with profitability during that period. Bank stocks plummeted, and our stock was no exception. I left in early 2011, as our bank began to lose its independence from Western Alliance.

Federal Reserve Bank of San Francisco

While I was at Alta Alliance, I was elected to a seat on the Twelfth District Federal Reserve Board, located in San Francisco. I held the seat designated for mid-sized community banks. There are twelve Federal Reserve districts, and our district covered California, Washington, Oregon, Nevada, Arizona, Alaska and Hawaii.

Janet Yellen, the current Secretary of the Treasury, was the President of the San Francisco Fed during most of my three-year term. At all meetings, she was clearly the smartest person in a room of smart people. One of our jobs was to give interest rate recommendations to The Federal Reserve Board in Washington D.C. Janet would begin with detailed recommendations, consisting of long paragraphs. When Janet gave an interest rate recommendation, there was typically not much discussion, and we ratified her conclusions.

One noteworthy responsibility we had was giving the economists in the room real-time data on economic activity in our communities. In discussing the Great Recession, we talked about the *scarring effect* the recession had on segments of our communities, similar to the Great Depression. During the Great Depression in the 1920s and early 30s, people were scarred for life, as families lost everything. During the great Recession, young people lost homes, middle-aged people lost their investments and retirement savings, and many of the wealthy had to scale back.

There was one metric that really dramatized the effect that the Great Recession had on ordinary people. One function of the 12 Federal Reserve Banks is to put new coins into the marketplace every quarter. During the fourth quarter of 2008, huge quantities of coins came back to the Fed. We thought most families had a coin jar where they kept excess coins accumulated during a typical day.

However, during the Great Recession, families were so broke that they used the coin in those jars to buy groceries, flooding supermarkets with coins, which in turn flooded banks with coin, which then flooded the 12 Federal Reserve banks with coin.

Tri-Valley Bank

After leaving Alta Alliance Bank, I spent a year in Chicago, trying to buy a troubled bank. There was no shortage of troubled banks in the Midwest during the Great Recession. I worked with a great investment banker, Robert (Bob) Kotecki, who has since passed. We looked at several banks, but we were not able to close a transaction.

When I returned to the Bay Area, I learned that Tri-Valley Bank in San Ramon, California, had experienced losses and was under pressure from the regulators to recapitalize. I put together another investor group, which was not easy, coming out of the Great Recession.

The original shareholders capitalized the bank at $10.00 a share. When we came in, the book was $2.50 a share and we recapped the bank at $.35 a share. I became Chairman, President, and CEO of the bank. We brought in   new directors, Robert Obana, Louis Cosso, Mark Lefanowicz, Guy Rounsaville, Regina Muehlhauser, and Scott McKinlay. We also brought in new C level officers, Glen Lezama, Chief Credit Officer, and Lisa Milke at first and Marshall Griffin subsequently as Chief Financial Officers. Our business plan included bringing low-cost deposits, and good performing loans into the bank. Five years later, we sold the bank to Heritage Bank of Commerce in San Jose for $.82 a share.

Chapter 9: Enjoy the Journey

"There are years that ask questions and there are years that answer." - Their Eyes Were Watching God, Zora Neale Hurston

In the mid-1990s, Wells Fargo sent me to a speech consultant who taught me that every successful executive has a *Pearls of Wisdom* speech in their back pocket—to be used if called on short notice to speak. I used this speech or a close variation of it for more than 5 years. It was especially useful when I was a faculty member at UCLA's Anderson School of Business African American Leadership Institute. For me, this original *emergency* speech has become a passion of mine-and has its own journey. Over the years, I have made minor updates to the speech to make it more relevant to today's world.

A version of the speech is as follows:

First, enjoying life, as a journey and not a destination, permeates everything that I am going to talk about and that includes:
> *The importance of imagination*
> *The importance of passion*
> *How do you get a mentor*
> *Why is it important to be a mentor?*
> *The importance of community service*
> *The importance of suffering*
> *Confronting one's bogeyman.*
> *Having a moral compass*
> *The importance of having a religious/spiritual base*

In addition to these topics, I have several books that I would like to share with you that have helped me on my journey. I believe that if you want to be successful, you must read everything. I will talk more about reading later.

A favorite book of mine is *The Alchemist*. It is a story of a young boy in search of his fortune. He goes all over the land looking for the pot of gold at the end of the rainbow. What he discovers toward the end of the book is that the treasure is in the journey.

Many of us spend too many years searching for that pot of gold before we understand that it is all about the journey. Some of us never get to that level of understanding. The common mistake that we all make is that we focus on getting to a place instead of enjoying the journey.

If only I could only make $200,000. If only I could make $500,000, my life would be okay. If I could become a regional manager... If I could become a general manager... If I could become a vice president, then I could relax and smell the roses.

Enjoying the journey means understanding what a gift the present is. Read *The Precious Present* by Spencer Johnson. In addition to our life journey is a higher-level journey that Howard Thurman talks about in his book, *The Inward Journey*. How many of you have heard of Howard Thurman? In *The Inward Journey*, Thurman speaks of is the journey to see God within us, and to then see God in others.

Enjoying the Journey, *Imagination*, and *Passion* deal with our ability to see God everywhere. The next three topics deal with our ability to see God in others and the last four topics deal with our ability to take the inward journey and see God within ourselves.

I believe that whether we are talking about our life journey or the inward journey, we are talking about our relationships with people around us, bosses, peers, subordinates, and our relationship with ourselves.

Imagination

What is imagination? Zora Neale Hurston captured the essence of imagination in her book, *Their Eyes Were Watching God*, when she said that "Some people can look at a mud puddle and see an ocean with ships."

Why do employers need any of us? It is because of our creativity and our imagination. *Technology can handle everything else. Secondly, if institutions have to reinvent themselves, as Artificial Intelligence and the Metiverse challenge conventional thinking, we have to challenge our historical assumptions and be able to reinvent ourselves.*

How does one grow the imaginative process? There are many ways. Five that I would focus on are as follows:

We need to read everything, especially fiction. We need to become proponents of lifelong learning, scrapping the concept of finishing our education. Fortune magazine once stated that people who read have that marvelous ability to see linkage between unrelated events. It's one of the most important qualities that a person can have. In general, the higher a person's reading skills, the higher his professional achievement.

Successful people that I know read one book a week, one to two daily newspapers and the Wall Street Journal, and one to two weekly magazines plus professional journals.

Next, have big dreams. There is no journey if you are already where you are going. I think that I can safely say that Artificial Intelligence (AI) has not developed the ability to dream.

The great religious philosopher, Howard Thurman, said, "Our dreams should be so large that we are constantly humbled by them." I believe that large dreams push us to be more imaginative. There is an essay in *Deep is the Hunger* by Howard Thurman that talks about the importance of having big dreams. There is a symbiotic relationship between big dreams and imagination that allows us to see a world that is greater and better than the one that we experience and live. *What are your dreams? My dream is to change the world.* I will explain later.

Next, learn how to fly. Push yourself outside of your comfort zone. Unburden yourself of the shackles of how you have done things in the past as a guide for how you should do things in the future. Read *Song of Solomon* by Toni Morrison. Morrison has the protagonist literally and figuratively learning how to fly. It has been said that sometimes you have to jump off a cliff and grow your wings on the way down. Remember that learning how to fly is understanding that "life is big."

Next, walk with elephants. Lloyd Ward the former Chairman of Maytag tells the fable of an elephant and an ant that were walking together in a forest. Their journey took them across a bridge. The bridge started to squeak and rumble. When they got to the other side, the ant said, "Boy we really shook that thing, didn't we!"

If you want to be creative, get to know creative people. Creative people have a way of expanding our limits.

Who are these elephants? Who are these creative people? I believe they tend to be, as the saying goes, people who "have seen the elephant, heard the owl, and have been to the other side of the mountain." These are people who have seen the breadth of life, grown through suffering, and experienced their own personal epiphany.

If you cannot personally know great people, read their works. Reading the works of the greats is a form of walking with elephants.

Finally, hear the omens. The young man in *The Alchemist* discovered that when he paid attention to the omens, more came his way. When he ignored the omens, fewer were available to him. I believe we see, hear, or internalize only a fraction of the information we experience on a daily basis that can help us with our journey.

As we become more sensitive to the information or messages that come to us, we are able to capture and process a larger percentage of those messages. This increased sensitivity to all the world shares with us can make us more imaginative.

Brent Staples in *Parallel Times* talks about the importance of carrying a journal. Many big thinkers carry journals so that they can capture much of the information, messages, and omens that the world brings to them on a daily basis. The more you capture, the larger your world grows, the greater the possibilities you see, and the more imaginative you become.

Again, read everything, have big dreams, learn to fly, walk with elephants, and hear the omens if you want to be more imaginative.

Discover your Passion.

Have you noticed that truly successful people have a certain look in their eye, they have a certain intensity, they work constantly, and they appear to be driven unlike the rest of us? One of the things that makes the great "great" is passion.

I believe that passion is the straw that stirs the drink for truly successful people. Without it, you can only go so far. Why do Steph Curry, Lebron James, Patrick Mahomes, Tiger Woods and others like them transcend their sports in ways that others cannot? Why does Elon Musk sit at the top of the corporate pyramid and manage to stay there while being besieged by enemies from every direction?

They all have an overriding passion and sense of purpose for what they do, and that passion becomes the yeast that combines all of their skills, knowledge, energy, and drive to transcend them above the crowd to accomplish their goals.

If you notice, people who have passion do not believe that they are working in the traditional sense. If you view work as "work," you can never become great. There have been times in my career that I have so enjoyed what I was doing that I could not believe that I was getting paid to do it. At the end of the day, I had to make myself go home.

> You cannot sustain intensity,
> You cannot consistently work long hours,
> You cannot be creative or have imagination if you do not have passion.

Octavia Butler in *Bloodchild* talks about what it means to be a great writer. It is not just about imagination, but the hard work of rewriting and rewriting lines of fiction until she is satisfied with a passage.

Ralph Ellison, author of *Invisible Man*, was notorious for being so passionate about his work that he constantly rewrote lines in search of the perfect passage. These people could not accomplish what they have accomplished if they viewed work as "work." They have obviously pursued their passion.

I once attended a Prince concert. Prince did not view work as work. If you have ever seen him, you know that you are in the presence of someone following their passion.

How do you find your passion? I believe that the same ways that you become imaginative helps you find your purpose and when you find your purpose, you find your passion.

Reading exposes you to a bigger world and helps you to find that activity or purpose that you must pursue.

Passionate people get used to living life on the edge. It has been said that living life on the edge allows you to see things that you might not see from the center. It has also been said that if you are not living life on the edge, you are taking up too much space.

Big dreams give you purpose and passion. If your dreams are big enough, they will consume you and cause you to be passionate about everything that is in pursuit of that dream.

Walking with elephants is critical. Spending time with the great can help you to find your passion.

How many times have we seen someone who was drifting have a door to their souls unlocked by spending time with the right person or reading the great works of the right person? Being confronted with omens (the burning bush) can push a person to a personal epiphany and force him to embrace a purpose that he cannot ignore.

I believe that part of our journey is finding our passion, searching for that consuming purpose or series of purposes that we were meant to pursue. It has been said that the two greatest days of your life are the day that you were born and the day that you find your purpose.

I believe that when you find your purpose, you find your passion. I believe that my purpose and my passion are tied to my "big dream." I said that my dream is to change the world and, as I said, I will explain shortly.

Mentorship

Why would anyone want to mentor us? Why would a busy person want to focus on our careers? Over the years, Dr. Price Cobbs has done the best job of anyone that I know of demystifying the mentoring process. He states that we must remember that bosses are people – just like us, and as such, they spend most of their time thinking about themselves and their problems. Those who understand this concept and consistently find or become the solution to their bosses' problems become important to their bosses.

It is natural to want to protect or mentor someone who is important to you. People who understand this concept not only find solutions to the problems of their immediate superiors, but they also become problem solvers for a variety of people in their lives. The most successful people I have known are people who have had multiple mentors, because they are in the habit of finding solutions and being helpful to many people around them.

Price states that since many of us are first-generation managers and the talk around our dinner tables was probably more sympathetic to workers than to bosses, we may not have been socialized to empathize with the problems of bosses. If we want to be mentored, if we want to be important to our bosses, and if we want bosses to think about our careers and our needs, we must learn how to consistently become the solution to our bosses' problems.

Why should you be a mentor? I believe that getting a mentor and being a mentor are one in the same. They both are about helping others.

Some of my most rewarding experiences have occurred when I tried to help or mentor someone who I thought had potential, but was struggling, and someone who I did not think could possibly help me.

I believe that sometimes you have to give the gift of who you are to someone without any thought of the return that you might receive. I believe that there is a richness that you add to your life when you use your resources to help someone else. The paradox is that when you give the gift of yourself or your resources to someone without any thought of the return, there is a return or payback that occurs over time, that is exponentially greater, in psychic and real terms, than anything that you could have imagined at the time of your gift.

Some of the people who I have helped are now in my life forever, and I am blessed to have them in my life. I tie this back to enjoying the journey, seeing God in ourselves and in others, and having big dreams. We never know if the person who we mentor might go on to do something that is world changing. We never know if the person who is influenced by our example might go on to do something great. That is how I believe that we change the world.

Octavia Butler, the great science fiction writer, talks about the power to influence others and events in her book, *The Parable of the Sower*. Her protagonist believes that "everything that you touch, you change, everything that you change, changes you."

So, whether you are a mentor or mentee, you have the ability and opportunity to "leave footprints in the sands of time." The common thread in getting or being a mentor is:

> enjoying the journey,
> helping other people,
> ministering to other people,
> minimizing self and maximizing service.

Two books that are helpful in understanding the mentorship process are *The Seven Spiritual Laws of Success* by Deepak Chopra and *Servant Leadership* by Robert K. Greenleaf.

Chopra says in his "law of giving" that if you want attention and appreciation, then learn to *give* attention and appreciation... the easiest way to get what you want is to help others to get what they want. Learn to ask the question "How can I help?" which comes from the spirit versus "What's in it for me?" which comes from the ego.

Robert Greenleaf insists that all great leaders are first servants. Remember, it was Martin Luther King Jr. who said, "We all can become great because we can all serve." Mother Teresa said that "if you serve, you will have peace." She actually said, "If you

pray, you will have faith, and if you have faith, you will love, and if you love you will serve, and if you serve, you will have peace."
Mentorship is about helping others and being of service to others.

Community Service

"You give little when you give of your possessions. It is when you give of yourself that you truly give." ~Kahlil Gibran

There are many obvious benefits of community service:
You are able to develop leadership skills,
You expand contacts,
You are able to hone public speaking skills,
You can find career opportunities through volunteering.
The real reason to get involved is that community service is part of enjoying the journey.

Again, the focus is minimizing self and maximizing service.
Again, it is a chance to dream the big dream.
Again, it is a chance to find both purpose and passion.

Again, it is a chance to develop mentors and mentees by helping both! You never know who is watching. You never know if a potential mentor is watching your service. You never know if someone that you help through a community organization becomes the one who does something special or world changing.
How do you change the world? You change yourself. Stephen Covey in Principle-Centered Leadership says that a true paradox is that we find ourselves when we lose ourselves in service.
Francis of Assisi said, "You don't change the world as much as you change *worlds*." When we become involved with community organizations, we have an opportunity to change worlds, especially the worlds of young people, and one of those worlds might one day change the world.
I get to community service, changing the world, and changing worlds through the Last Mile Foundation, which awards grants

to students who find themselves at the college of their choice, but who are $500 to $2,000 short of registering.

We fund that gap. The only requirement of the student is that they write an essay in response to, *What is your dream? And how do you change the world and how are they related?* A portion of the revenues from Grisham Group fund the foundation.

Read *The Measure of My Success* by Marion Wright Edelman, who states that "Service, like community service, is the rent that we pay for living. It is the very purpose of life, not something that you do in your spare time."

So for me, through the Last Mile Foundation, I am paying rent, and I am trying to change the world, and this journey is changing me. Remember the parable of the sower — everything that you touch, you change, and everything that you change changes you.

Suffering

"The deeper that sorrow carves into your being, the more joy you can contain." ~Kahlil Gibran, The Prophet

One of the problems in hiring young people is that many have not yet had the opportunity to suffer. Typically, when I am in the presence of someone who is self-absorbed, I immediately think that the person probably has not had an opportunity to suffer. No one wants to suffer, but there is a certain perspective that unearned suffering brings to a life.

Why is trouble important? It is certainly inevitable. As biblical Job spoke, "Man born of woman is of few days and full of trouble." Trouble rains on the just as well as the unjust. There is trouble in corporate life, because there is trouble in life.

What happens when you hit the glass ceiling?

What happens when you do not get the promotion that you deserve?

What happens when racism rears its ugly head?

What happens when you get laid off or downsized?

What happens when you and your spouse no longer share the same dream?

What happens when personal tragedy occurs?

My experience is that one of two things occurs when trouble and the inevitable suffering occur. People become either bitter and inwardly focused, or they grow. Martin Luther King Jr. believed that unearned suffering is redemptive. Howard Thurman believed that suffering opens doors. In his book, *Disciplines of the Spirit*, he says that "openings are made in a life by suffering that are not made in any other way."

I believe that some of those doors that are opened by suffering that Thurman talks about lead to our imagination and passion.

> *Doors that crystallize and clarify our dreams.*
> *Doors to help us to learn how to fly.*

Doors that allow us to hear, see and experience the omens in our lives. Doors that allow us to better understand the importance of "walking with elephants" and understand the price that "elephants" have paid.

How many times have you seen someone:
1. Go through some incredibly tragic experience?
2. Have that experience redefine who they are?
3. State that the experience was critical to their growth and who they now are?

Magic Johnson might not have become such the positive, community-minded entrepreneur in the Black community had he not been diagnosed with HIV. Note that he did not become bitter or inwardly focused. One might go so far as to say that HIV opened doors of service for Magic, since absent his HIV diagnosis, the door might not have opened to cause him to be the community-minded entrepreneur that his has become.

The prayer below captures the essence of the importance of suffering.

Answered Prayer

Author Unknown

I asked for strength, that I might achieve,
I was made weak, that I might learn humbly to obey...
I asked for health, that I might do greater things,
I was given infirmity, that I might do better things...
I asked for riches, that I might be happy,
I was given poverty, that I might be wise...
I asked for power, that I might have the praise of men,
I was given weakness, that I might feel the need of God...
I asked for all things, that I might enjoy life,
I was given life, that I might enjoy all things...
I got nothing that I asked for – but everything that I hoped for;
Almost despite myself, my unspoken prayers were answered.
I am among all men, most richly blessed.

Confronting your Bogeyman

"Why are ye fearful, oh ye of little faith?" (Mat. 8:26)

We all have a bogeyman. Careers today require so many skills that it is difficult to excel in every activity that we need to excel. Everyone has some inadequacy that they are trying to hide. I call that inadequacy our bogeyman.

For some people, their bogeyman may be math; for others, writing; for others, the computer; and others, selling. For some people, their bogeyman is change. Spencer Johnson's *Who Moved My Cheese?* is a great parable about learning to get over the fear of change. Cheese can be a metaphor for those skills that represent our strengths. A form of learning how to fly is learning to go after new cheese... develop new strengths.

My bogeyman has always been public speaking, and I have had to confront that bogeyman many times throughout my life. There have been times when I have been sitting in an audience, waiting to be introduced, and my anxiety has been so high that I thought I was going to die, and no one would know why. I have been on the verge of a full-on panic attack prior to many speeches. I literally have had to remind myself that I am a child of God and that everything will be okay.

My experience is that most people have a need to hide what scares them. People do not realize that everyone fears some perceived inadequacy. People tend to think that they are the only ones that are apprehensive about something. Everyone who you meet is afraid of something.

There is a passage in Coelho's *The Alchemist* that reads:

> *"My heart is afraid that it will have to suffer,"* the boy told the Alchemist one night as they looked up at the moonless sky.
> *Tell your heart that the fear of suffering is worse than the suffering itself. And that no heart has ever suffered when it goes in search of its dreams.*

Confronting your bogeyman means moving beyond your fears, if you want to enjoy the journey. Spencer Johnson in *Who Moved My Cheese?* says that you have to recognize your fears and move beyond them if you want to be free. He asks the question, "What would you do if you were not afraid?" What are the great things that we all might do if we were not afraid.

I have found that you must force yourself to confront your bogeyman if you want to grow, personally and professionally. You have to yank back the covers from what is scaring you. It is the only way to turn a weakness into a strength. We tend to focus on our strengths, making them stronger, while avoiding our weaknesses, allowing them to become weaker.

I have seen people take themselves "out of the game" and out of competition for jobs because they refuse to put themselves at risk and "confront their bogeyman." Steven Pressfield in *The*

Legend of Bagger Vance, say through his protagonist that "there is one battle [in our lives] ... and we are compelled by our nature... to fight it again and again."

"Confronting your bogeyman" is a metaphor for the battle in our lives that we fight over and over again. What is it that you are afraid that you battled in the past, are currently battling and are preparing to battle in the future?

Public speaking is the battleground where I battle my fears. I have battled it in the past, I am battling it as I stand here today, and I prepare to battle it in the future, and I will win.

I have found that you are not living life when you run from your fears and try to take the risk or uncertainty out of your life."

Dennis Kimbro, in *What Makes the Great Great*, quotes Pericles, who said, "The secret of happiness is freedom, and the secret of freedom is courage."

Stephen Covey, author of *The Seven Habits of Highly Effective People*, states that "the greatest risk is the risk of riskless living.

I believe that in order to enjoy the journey and experience the exhilaration of life, you have to continually put yourself at risk, face the abyss, and form a personal relationship with your bogeyman.

And for my own bogeyman, which is public speaking, I have learned that my bogeyman is God's way of reminding me that I cannot make this journey by myself.

Another way of looking at imagination, passion, mentorship, community service and confronting our bogeyman as roadmaps to changing the world is summed up in Marianne Williamson's *Our Deepest Fear* essay:

Our deepest fear is not that we are inadequate. Our deepest fear is that we are powerful beyond measure. It is our light, not our darkness, that most frightens us.

We ask ourselves, 'Who am I to be brilliant, gorgeous, talented, fabulous?' Actually, who are you not to be? You are a child of God.

Your playing small does not serve the world. There is nothing enlightened about shrinking so that other people won't feel insecure around you.

We were born to make manifest the glory of God that is within us. It's not just in some of us; it's in everyone. And as we let our own light shine, we unconsciously give other people permission to do the same. As we are liberated from our own fear, our presence automatically liberates others.

Moral Compass

If you want to be great, or if you want to change the world, you better have a moral compass. If you are an African American and you just want to be moderately successful, you better have a moral compass. What is a moral compass? It is that inner voice that defines right from wrong.

Regardless of how subtle the issues,
Regardless of how high the stakes,
Regardless of how much money is on the table,
A moral compass, an inner voice or a feeling in the gut is what we must have in order to avoid trouble.

Stephen Covey says in *Principle-Centered Leadership* that a moral compass tells you where True North lies. In *What Makes the Great Great?* Dennis Kimbro says, "Character is what you are in the dark."

Many successful journeys have been derailed because the individual who had tremendous potential or technical skills also had some moral deficiency. As African Americans, we are held to a higher standard than our majority counterparts. When anyone rises above the crowd, a hot spotlight begins to zero in, looking for weakness; it is more intense for African Americans.

It seems that every day we read about some corporate executive who thought he was above the law. I believe Donald Trump and his enablers are being disgraced for not having moral compasses.

You do not have to commit a crime be tarnished by the perception of wrongdoing. It is interesting how many people are brought down for just the perception of wrongdoing.

The more successful we become, or the more that we try to change the world, the more intense the spotlight becomes, the higher the morality bar is raised, and the more finely tuned our moral compass must be.

There was a series in the *New York Times* about Las Vegas. One of the legends of the town, Jack Binion has been quoted as saying, "Las Vegas was the best town to live in if you have no weaknesses—but if you have one, we'll find it." Moving up in corporate America can be great too, but if you have any moral weaknesses they will be found. Ask all the folks that have taken perp-walks.

Expect to be investigated and scrutinized, if you have big dreams, if you want to be great or if you want to change the world.

Remember that a finely-tuned moral compass, with a keen sense of where True North lies, helps us to not only avoid wrongdoing, but the higher test—the perception of wrongdoing.

Religious/Spiritual Base

This is very personal, and I am not suggesting that what I am going to say next applies to anyone other than me, but as James Baldwin once said, "In order to have a conversation with someone, you must reveal yourself." This is my attempt to reveal myself to you.

When I think of the importance of having a religious/spiritual base, I think of an old spiritual that begins, "My soul looks back and wonders, how I got over."

I could not have come this far if it were not for my faith. In the middle of the night when everything about my career has seemed dismal and bleak, knowing as Job once said, that my redeemer lives has given me the strength to see a new day.

When trouble and its cousin, suffering, invariably come, you can either run away, break, or have a belief system that says *whatever doesn't kill me will make me stronger*. When you look at people like me, it is easy to see the successes. Less apparent are the struggles and how I have gotten through them.

How my faith has played out in my life:

- When a very influential professor in college told me that I wasn't grad school material, I persevered anyway, because I knew my redeemer lived.
- When I was passed over for promotions at a major bank in Chicago in the 1970s and I fought the bitterness that so many African American males succumb to – I knew my redeemer lived.
- When I was told that I could not have a European assignment by the same bank because Europeans were not ready to accept African Americans, I was still able to fight bitterness, because I knew my redeemer lived.
- When I had an opportunity to escape this business (and everyone here knows that we didn't have many opportunities to switch companies), I was offered a top management job by a European bank (headquartered in Chicago) and had it rescinded because my new subordinates said they could not work for me – a Black man, I knew by redeemer lived.
- When I had to convince my wife with tears in her eyes to come to a land that was not part of her dreams, so that I could avoid the overt discrimination of Chicago, I was sustained, because I knew my redeemer lived.
- When Carl Reichardt, Chairman of Wells Fargo Bank, called and said the Board of Directors of Wells Fargo Bank had elected me as an executive vice president and I felt unworthy, because I knew so many other African Americans who have worked harder than me, are smarter than me and have shed more blood that I have – but have been denied opportunity, I was sustained because I knew my redeemer lived.
- When I made the decision to leave Wells Fargo because the new acquirer, Norwest, did not understand who I was or why they needed me, and the next day, the Chairman of a local community bank called and asked if I would be *their* new

President, I knew once again that I was not alone on my journey and that my redeemer lived.

- When Korn/Ferry called and said that it was time for me to run with the "big dogs" again, I knew that I needed to step up to a bigger purpose, and I began a new journey that has led to Grisham Group Executive Search and The Last Mile Foundation.

- When I read our Last Mile Foundation first scholarship recipient's essay and heard him say that "my mother is my commander, and I just want to succeed for her, given all that she has been through," I knew I was on the path to changing the world and that I had been forever changed too. "Everything that you touch, you change, and everything that you change, changes you."

- When the doctors told Jane that she only had six months to live, and the God above said, "Only I know when anyone in this life will transition to the next life," and she lived for five years, we knew our redeemer lived.

- When the God above gave me a new mate (Paulina Rosa Van) to continue on my journey and join her on her journey, I was once again reminded that my redeemer lived.

Given all that has been given to me – the least I can do is:

> Enjoy the journey!
> Have purpose and passion!
> Try to be a mentor!
> Immerse myself in community service!
> And try to change the world.

I must do all these things because in the middle of the night, "when my soul looks back and wonders how I got over," I have the luxury of being able to remember that "I know my redeemer lives."

In 1999, I had just been named President of a local bank. Also, I was on the faculty at the African American Leadership Institute at the Anderson School of Management at UCLA. After giving a variation of my speech. I was interviewed by the Institute for their newsletter.

Participant: As you continue to make your transition in your new position as a bank president, what do you foresee as being your greatest leadership challenge?

ATG: I believe that one of the greatest leadership challenges for many of us—once we have we reached this stage—is trying to determine how we can leave footprints in the sand. How can we become an instrument of positive change? How do we set an example to encourage others to contribute to the greater good?

I am very excited about not only what I can do to grow my own organization, but how I can use this platform to continue to affect positive change?

In a recent interview with the *San Francisco Business Journal*, the reporter had questioned me on many different topics. However, the theme that the reporter chose to write about was my view on the importance of community service. I insisted in the article that I was committed to community service and that commitment extended to my time and money. I also stated that I wanted to encourage other executives to commit their time along with corporate and personal funds to community service.

Participant: Given this challenge, do you anticipate implementing a different leadership style?

ATG: What I am finding inside and outside of my organization, is that it is important for me to lead by example, and with a great deal of humility, because of the perception of the position (President). Being an Executive Vice President at Wells Fargo Bank was an important position. However, being a President of a regional bank is a highly visible position, and I am conscious that many are watching my example. We should always be conscious of our style and behaviors, because we never know when the world is watching.

Participant: Any final thoughts/words of advice?

ATG: Especially for MBAs—if your dreams are only about power, position and money, "at the end of the day" you will be very disappointed because you will find that your dreams are too small. And you will find that you have a great deal of emptiness in your life.

African - American Leadership Institute, Fall 1998

Chapter 10: Rare Book Collection

"There are many wonderful things that will never get done, if you do not do them." ~ *Charles Gill*

As you can see, my world is awash in numbers. As a Black man, I had to overcome racial and cultural obstacles to become successful, but as I became older, I realized I knew little about my own culture's history and thought.

I began to remedy that during my term as chairman of Wells Fargo's Cultural Diversity Committee. I was fortunate that Oakland and Berkeley had so many rare and eclectic bookstores, where I could browse and discover. There was something special about reading a first edition of African American fiction, nonfiction, or poetry that called to me and drew me into the work.

Slowly but earnestly, I became a collector. It was my way of owning my history and culture, and of finding my way. My first rare book was a 1927 edition of *The Autobiography of an Ex Colored Man* by James Weldon Johnson. That was followed by first editions of *Native Son* by Richard Wright and *Cabin and Field* by Paul Dunbar. Recent first editions include both of Barack Obama's first books, signed in the White House.

My favorite pre-Harlem Renaissance fiction writer is James Weldon Johnson. My favorite Harlem Renaissance writer, besides Richard Wright, is Zora Neale Hurston, because of her book, *Their Eyes Were Watching God*.

First editions of works by James Baldwin, Cyrus Colter, and Toni Morrison hold special places in my collection and consciousness. With the new interest in Afrofuturism, I am pleased to own a signed, first edition of *Kindred*, the extraordinary book by Octavia Butler, the Dean of Afrofuturism.

My library includes poems from Countee Cullen and Langston Hughes, pictures from photojournalist Gordon Parks, allegories from Derrick Bell, satire from Ishmael Reed, inspirational commentary from W.E.B. DuBois, and spiritual enlightenment from Howard Thurman. His *Deep is the Hunger, Meditations of the Heart,* and *The Inward Journey* are a trilogy of essays that I believe are classics.

Jane and I had over 1,000 books between our homes in Oakland and Chicago. In 2016, we donated 500 first editions to the DePaul University John T. Richardson Library. The library was relatively new and had a very sophisticated rare book section within its overall collection. Most of the books that we donated were signed and inscribed to us by the authors.

Father Utivec, a senior administrator and educator within DePaul, supervised the library. He had a previous interest in rare African American books and had started a collection. I believe that the addition of our collection to Father Utivec's created one of the largest assemblages of rare African American books in the country.

In valuing our books, we were introduced to the concept of provenance. In rare art, book, and other similar collections, a collection or "provenance" has its own unique history and value that is different, typically greater than the sum of the individual books. DePaul's John T. Richardson Library had a reception after the University trustee meeting in May 2017 to showcase the collection (see below).

DePaul
UNIVERSITY

You and a guest are cordially invited to a private
viewing of the Arnold and Jane Grisham Collection

Thursday, May 18
6 p.m. to 7:30 p.m.

John T. Richardson Library
Special Collections
2350 N. Kenmore Avenue, Room 314
Chicago

Space is limited. Please respond no later than Thursday, May 11 by calling
the Office of Advancement at (312) 362-8455 or emailing
eventRSVP@depaul.edu. Please indicate any special needs or
dietary restrictions in your response.

Arnold and Jane Grisham Collection

The Arnold and Jane Grisham collection displays the breadth of African American literature from the early poems of Paul Laurence Dunbar to the modern mystery novels of Walter Mosley. The Collection is a prime resource for students engaged in critical analysis of changes to the African American literary canon or researching key literary moments such as the Harlem and Chicago Renaissances and the birth of Afrofuturism. The collection also represents the voices of many African American women and is a particularly good resource for research at the intersection of race and gender. Although the majority of the text fall into literature and fiction, the collection has a multidisciplinary scope and also contains books on black political thought, theology, fine arts, and history.

Author	Book	Year Published	Edition
Achebe, Chinua	Arrow of God	1964	1st UK
Achebe, Chinua	Hopes and Impediments	1989	1st
Achebe, Chinua	Morning Yet On Creation Day	1975	1st
Achebe, Chinua	There was a Country	2012	1st
Akpan, Uwem	Say You're One of Them	2008	1st
Alexander, Adele Logan	Homelands and Waterways	1999	1st
Alexander, Eleanor	Lyrics of Sunshine and Shadow	2001	
Alexander, Lydia Lewis; etal	Wearing Purple	1996	1st
Allen, Jeffery	Rails Under my Back	2000	1st
Alter, Jonathan	The Center Holds: Obama and His Enemies.	2013	1st
Anderson & Byrne	Brown v. Board of Education	2004	1st
Angelou, Maya	All God's Children Need Traveling Shoes	1986	1st signed
Angelou, Maya	Even the Stars Look Lonesome	1997	1st signed
Angelou, Maya	The Heart of a Woman	1981	1st
Angelou, Maya	I Know Why the Caged Bird Sings	1997	inscribed
Angelou, Maya	I Shall Not Be Moved	1990	1st
Angelou, Maya	Oh Pray My Wings Are Gonna Fit Me Well	1975	1st
Angelou, Maya	Singin' and Swingin and getting Merry Like Christmas	1976	1st
Angelou, Maya	Wouldn't Take Nothing For My Journey Now	1993	1st
Archibald, Chestina Mitchell	Say Amen	1997	1st
Ashe, Arthur	Days of Grace	1993	1st
Ashe, Jr, Arthur	A Hard Road To Glory 1919-1945	1988	1st
Ashe, Jr, Arthur	A Hard Road To Glory Since 1946	1988	1st
Baker, Calvin	Dominion	2006	
Baldwin, James	Another Country	1963	1st UK
Baldwin, James	The Devil Finds Work	1976	1st
Baldwin, James	The Evidence of Things Not Seen	1985	1st
Baldwin, James	The Fire Next Time	1963	1st
Baldwin, James	Giovanni's Room	1956	1st
Baldwin, James	Going To Meet The Man	1965	1st
Baldwin, James	If Beale Street Could Talk	1974	1st
Baldwin, James	Just Above My Head	1978	1st
Baldwin, James	Nobody Knows My Name	1961	1st UK
Baldwin, James	No Name in the Street	1972	1st
Baldwin, James	The Price of the Ticket	1985	1st
Baldwin, James	Tell me how long the train's been gone	1968	1st
Baldwin/Mead	A Rap on Race	1971	1st
Bascom, Lionel C	A Renaissance in Harlem	1999	1st
Baxter, Freddie Mae	The Seventh Child	1999	
Bell, Derrick	And We Are Not Saved	1987	1st
Bell, Derrick	Confronting Authority	1994	1st signed
Bell, Derrick	Ethical Ambition	2002	1st signed
Bell, Derrick	Faces At The Bottom Of The Well	1992	1st signed
Bell, Derrick	Gospel Choirs	1996	1st
Bennett, Lerone Jr	Before the Mayflower	1992	25th Annive
Bennett, Lerone Jr	Forced Into Glory	1999	3rd
Berlin, Ira, etal.	Remembering Slavery	1998	
Berry, Faith	Before and Beyond Harlem	1983	
Berry, Leonidas	I Wouldn't Take Nothin' For My Journey	1981	1st
Billingsley, Andrew	Climbing Jacob's Ladder	1992	1st signed
Black, Timuel D. Jr	Bridges of Memory	2003	1st
Bland, Eleanor Taylor	A Cold and Silent Dying	2004	1st, inscribe
Bland, Eleanor Taylor	Windy City Dying	2002	1st, inscribe
Branch, Taylor	At Canaan's Edge	2006	1st
Branch, Taylor	Parting the Waters	1988	
Branch, Taylor	Pillar of Fire	1998	1st signed
Briscoe, Connie	Big Girls Don't Cry	1996	1st
Briscoe, Connie	A Long Way from Home	1999	1st
Brooks, Gwendolyn	Maud Martha	1951	1st
Brown, Claude	Manchild in the Promiseland	1965	1st
Broyard, Bliss	One Drop	2007	1st
Burnett, Whit	Black Hands on a White Face	1971	
Butler, Octavia E.	Blood Child	1995	1st
Butler, Octavia E.	Dawn	1987	1st
Butler, Octavia E.	Fledgling	2005	1st inscribe
Butler, Octavia E.	Imago	1989	1st
Butler, Octavia E.	Kindred	1979	1st signed
Butler, Octavia E.	Mind of My Mind	1977	1st signed
Butler, Octavia E.	Parable of the Sower	1993	1st
Butler, Octavia E.	Parable of the Talents	1998	1st signed
Butler, Octavia E.	Wild Seed	1980	1st

Campbell, Bebe Moore	72 Hour Hold	2004 1st
Campbell, Bebe Moore	Brothers and Sisters	1994 1st
Campbell, Bebe Moore	Singing in the Comeback Choir	1998 1st inscribe
Campbell, Bebe Moore	Sweet Summer	1989 1st
Carney, Vaughn A.	Swiss Movement	1998
Carroll, Rebecca	I know what the Red Clay Looks Like	Galley
Carroll, Rebecca	Swing Low	Galley
Carson and Holloran	A Knock at Midnight: Inspirations from the Sermons of Reverend Martin	1998 1st
Carson, Clayborne	The Papers of Martin Luther King, Jr Vol III	1997 1st, inscribe
Cary, Lorene	The Price of a Child	1995 1st
Chambers, Veronica	Mama's Girl	1996 1st
Chase-Riboud, Barbara	Echo of Lions	1989 1st
Chase-Riboud, Barbara	Portrait of a Nude Woman as Cleopatra	1987 galley
Chase-Riboud, Barbara	The President's Daughter	1994 1st
Chase-Riboud, Barbara	Sally Hemings	1979 1st
Cleage, Pearl	Deals with the Devil	1993 1st
Cleaver, Eldridge	Soul on Ice	1968 1st
Clinton, Catherine	Harriet Tubman	2004
Cobbs, Price	Black Rage	1968 1st inscribe
Cobbs, Price	Cracking the Corporate Code	2003 1st inscribe
Cobbs, Price	My American Life	2005 1st inscribe
Collins, Charles M	The African Americans	1993 1st inscribe
Collins, Charles M	A Day in the Life of Africa	2002 1st signed
Colter, Cyrus	The Amoralists	1988 Galley
Colter, Cyrus	A Chocolate Soldier	1988 Galley
Colter, Cyrus	City of Light	1993 1st inscribe
Colter, Cyrus	The Rivers of Eros	1972 1st
Colter,Cyrus	Beach Umbrella	1970 1st signed
Colter,Cyrus	The Hippodrome	1973 1st
Colter,Cyrus	Night Studies	1979 1st
Comer, James P.	Maggie's American Dream	1988 1st
Cooper, J. California	The Future Has A Past	2000 1st signed
Cooper, J. California	In Search of Satisfaction	1994 1st
Cooper, J. California	Life is Short but Wide	2009 4th signed
Cooper, J. California	The Matter is Life	1991 1st
Cooper, J. California	Same People, Same Other Place	2004 1st
Cooper, J. California	The Wake of the Wind	1998 1st signed
Cose, Ellis	A Man's World	1995 1st
Cose, Ellis	The Rage of a Privileged Class	1993 1st
Courlander, Harold	A Treasury of African American Folklore	1996 2nd
Cross, June	Secret Daughter: A Mixed Race Daughter and the Mother Who Gave He	2006 1st
Cullen, Countee	Caroling Dusk	1927 1st
Cullen, Countee	Color	1st
Cullen, Countee	Copper Sun	1927 1st
Cullen, Countee	One Way To Heaven	1932 1st
Cummings, George C.L.	A Common Journey	1993
Cummings, George C.L. and Dwight I	Cut Loose Your Stammering Tongue	1991 inscribed
Cuthbert, Margaret	Silent Cradle	1998 1st inscribe
Dance, Daryl Cumber	Honey, Hush!	1998 1st
Danticat, Edwidge	Breath, Eyes, Memory	1994 1st
Danticat, Edwidge	Brother, I'm Dying	2007 1st signed
Danticat, Edwidge	Claire of the Sea Light	2013 1st signed
Danticat, Edwidge	The Dew Breaker	2001 1st inscribe
Davis, Benjamin O.	An Autobiography of Benjamin O. Davis	1991 1st
Davis, Ossie and Ruby Dee	With Ossie and Ruby	1998 1st signed
Decosta-Willis, Miriam	Memphis Diary of Ida B. Wells	1995
Dove, Rita	Fifth Sunday	1985 1st
Dove, Rita	Grace Notes	1989 1st
Dove, Rita	Mother Love	1995 1st
Dove, Rita	Thomas and Beulah	1986 1st
Dove, Rita	Through the Ivory Gate	1992 1st
Dove, Rita	The Yellow House on the Corner	1989 2nd
Du Bois, W. E. B.	Mansart Builds A School	1959 1st
Du Bois, W. E. B.	The Ordeal of Mansart	1957 1st
Du Bois, W. E. B.	WEB Du Bois Reader	1970 1st
Du Bois, W. E. B.	Worlds Of Color	1961 1st
Due, Tananarive	The Between	1995 Galley
Due, Tananarive	The Living Blood	2001
Due, Tananarive	My Soul To Keep	1997 1st
Dunbar, Paul Laurence	Li'l Gal	1904 4th
Dunbar, Paul Laurence	Poems of Cabin and Field	1895 2nd
Dunbar, Paul Laurence	The Uncalled	1898 1st

Ellison, Ralph	Flying Home and Other Stories	1996	1st
Ellison, Ralph	Going To The Territory	1986	1st
Ellison, Ralph	Juneteenth	1999	1st
Ellison, Ralph	Shadow & Act	1964	1st
Ellison, Ralph	Trading Twelves	2000	1st
Etheridge, Eric	Breach of Peace		1st
Everett, Percival	Erasure		1st
Falkner, David	Great Time Coming	1995	1st
Farley, Christopher John	My Favorite War	1996	1st
Farmer, James	Lay Bare the Heart	1985	1st inscribe
Fidelman, Geoffrey Mark	First Lady of Song: Ella Fitzgerald for the Record	1994	1st
Fisher, Antwone Quenton	Finding Fish	2001	1st
Forrest, Leon	Divine Days	1992	1st signed
Forrest, Leon	Meteor in the Madhouse	2001	1st
Forrest, Leon	Relocations of the Spirit	1994	1st
Forrest, Leon	There is a Tree More Ancient than Eden	1973	1st
Forrest, Leon	Two Wings to Veil My Face	1983	1st
Franklin, John Hope	The Color Line	1993	1st
Franklin, John Hope	George Washington Williams	1985	
Franklin, V. P.	Living Our Stories	1995	1st
Frederick D Peterson Research Instit	The African American Education Data Book Volume 1,2 & 3	1997	1st
French, Albert	Billy	1993	1st signed
French, Albert	Holly	1995	1st
French, Albert	I Can't Wait On God	1998	1st
French, Albert	Patches of Fire	1997	1st
Gaines, Ernest J	A Gathering of Old Men	1983	1st signed
Gaines, Patrice	Laughing in the Dark	1994	Galley
Gaines, Patrice	Moments of Grace	1997	1st
Gardner, Chris	Pursuit of Happyness	2006	1st
Gates & West	The African American Century	2000	1st
Gates & West	The Future of the Race	1996	1st
Gates, Henry Louis	Colored People	1994	1st
Gates/Hannah Crafts	The Bondwoman's Narrative	2002	1st
Gates/McKay	African American Literature	1997	1st
Gautier, Amina	At-Risk	2011	1st
Gibson, Bob	Stranger to the Game	1994	1st
Gillead, LeRoy F.	The Tuskegee Experiment and Tuskegee Airmen, 1939-1949	1994	signed
Giovanni, Nikki	Love Poems	1997	1st
Giovanni, Nikki	Quilting The Black-Eyed Pea	2002	1st signed
Gomes, Peter	The Good Book	1996	1st
Gomes, Peter	Sermons	1998	1st
Greer, Robert	The Devil's Backbone	1998	1st
Greer, Robert	The Devil's Hatband	1996	1st signed
Greer, Robert	The Devil's Red Nickel	1997	1st signed
Grier, William H., and Price M. Co	The Jesus Bag	1971	1st signed
Guinier, Lani	The Tyranny Of The Majority	1994	1st
Habila, Helon	Waiting for an Angel	2002	1st
Haley, Alex	A Different Kind of Christmas	1988	1st
Haley, Alex	Roots	1976	1st
Haygood, Will	King of the Cats	1993	
Heilemann, John, and Mark Halperin	Game Change: Obama and the Clintons, McCain and Palin, and the Race	2010	1st
Hemenway, Robert E.	Zora Neale Hurston: A Literary Biography	1977	
Himes, Chester	The Heat's On	1986	UK Edition
Himes, Chester	A Rage In Harlem	1957	UK Edition
Hine, Darlene Clark	A Shining Thread of Hope	1998	1st
Holton, Hugh	Criminal Element	2002	1st
Holton, Hugh	The Devil's Shadow	2001	1st
Holton, Hugh	The Left Hand Of God	1999	1st
Holton, Hugh	Presumed Dead	1994	1st signed
Holton, Hugh	Red Lightning	1998	1st
Holton, Hugh	Revenge	2008	1st
Holton, Hugh	Time of the Assassins	2000	1st
Howard, Ravi	Like Trees, Walking	2007	1st
Hughes, Langston	Black Misery	1969	1st
Hughes, Langston	The Langston Huges Reader	1958	1st
Hughes, Langston	The Panther and theLash	1967	1st
Hughes, Langston	Simple Speaks His Mind	1950	1st
Hughes, Langston	Simple Stakes A Claim	1957	1st
Hughes, Langston	Tambourines To Glory	1958	1st
Hughes, Langston and Gloria Naylor	he Best Short Stories by Black Writers 1899-1967 ; Children of the Night	2002	1st
Hurston, Lucy Ann	Speak, So You Can Speak Again- The Life of Zora Neale Hurston	2004	1st
Ifill, Gwen	The Breakthrough: Politics and Race in the Age of Obama	2009	1st

Ilibagiza, Immaculee	Left to Tell: Discovering God Amidst the Rwandan Holocaust	2006	1st
Jackson, Brian Keith	Walking Through Mirrors	1998	1st
James, Etta	Rage to Survive	1995	1st
Johnson, Charles	Dreamer	1998	1st
Johnson, Charles	Dr King's Refrigerator	2005	1st
Johnson, Charles	Faith and the Good Thing	1974	1st
Johnson, Charles	Turning the Wheel	2003	1st
Johnson, Guy	Standing at the Scratch Line	1998	1st
Johnson, James Weldon	Autobiography of an Ex-Colored Man	1927	1st
Johnson, John H.	Succeeding Against the Odds	1989	1st inscribe
Jones, Edward	The Known World	2003	1st inscribe
Jones, Edward	Lost in the City	1992	1st
Jones, James Earl	Voices and Silences	1993	1st
Jordan, June	I was lookingat the ceiling and then I saw the sky	1995	1st
Jordan, June	Naming Our Destiny	1989	1st
Jordan, June	Soldier	2000	1st
Jordan, June	Technical Difficulties	1992	1st
Jordan, June	Who Look at Me	1969	1st
Jordan, Vernon	Vernon Can Read	2001	1st signed
Kantor, Jodi	The Obamas	2012	1st
Killens, John Oliver	Black Man's Burden	1965	1st signed
Killens, John Oliver	Cotillion	1971	1st
Killens, John Oliver	A Man Ain't Nothin But A Man	1975	1st
Killens, John Oliver	Youngblood	1954	1st
Kincaid, Jamaica	Annie John	1985	1st
Kincaid, Jamaica	At The Bottom of the River	1983	1st
Kincaid, Jamaica	The Autobiography of my Mother	1996	Galley
Kincaid, Jamaica	Lucy	1990	1st signed
Kincaid, Jamaica	Mr. Potter	2002	1st
Kincaid, Jamaica	My Brother	1997	1st
King, BB	The BB King Treasures	2005	1st
King, Coretta Scott (editor)	The Martin Luther King, Jr. Companion	1993	1st
King, Martin Luther	The Autobiography of Martin Luther King, Jr.	1998	1st, inscribe
King, Martin Luther	I Have a Dream	1993	
King, Martin Luther	I've Been to the Mountaintop	1994	
King, Martin Luther	Letter from the Birmingham Jail	1994	
Kissin, Eva H	Stories in Black and White	1970	1st
Kloppenberg, James T.	Reading Obama : dreams, hope, and the American political tradition	2011	1st
Komunyakaa, Yusef	Dien Cai Dau	1988	1st
Komunyakaa, Yusef	Lost in the Bonewheel Factory	1978	1st
Komunyakaa, Yusef	Magic City	1992	1st
Komunyakaa, Yusef	Neon Vernacular	1993	1st
Kotun, Debo	Abiku	1998	1st
Lamar, Jake	Bourgeois Blues	1991	1st
Lamar, Jake	The Last Integrationist	1996	Galley
Lamming, George	In The Castle Of My Skin	1953	1st
Lamming, George	Natives of my Person	1972	1st
Lamming, George	Water with Berries	1971	1st
Lawrence, Beverly Hall	Reviving the Spirit	1996	1st
Lawrence-Lightfoot, Sara	I've Known Rivers	1994	Galley
Lee, George L	Inspiring African Americans	1991	inscribed
Lee, George L	Worldwide Interesting People	1992	inscribed
Lee, George L	Interesting People	1976	1st signed
Leeming, David	James Baldwin: A Biography	1994	1st
Lefanu, Sarah and Stephen Hayward	Colours of a New Day	1990	
Lerner, Michael and Cornell West	Jews & Blacks	1995	1st inscribe
Lewis, David Levering	Harlem Renaissance Reader	1994	
Lewis, David Levering	W.E.B. DuBois Reader	2000	1st
Long, Richard	Black Writers and the American Civil War	1988	
Louie, Regina	Somebody's Someone	2003	1st signed
Louis, Joe	Joe Louis: My Life	1978	1st
Mandela, Nelson	Long Walk to Freedom	1994	1st
Marable, Manning	Malcolm X: A Life of Reinvention	2011	
Maraniss, David	Barack Obama: The Story	2012	1st
Massaquoi, Hans J	Destined to Witness	1999	1st
Maynard, Robert C	Letters To My Children	1995	1st
McBride, James	The Good Lord Bird	2013	1st
McBride, James	The Color of Water: A Black Man's Tribute to His White Mother	1995	Galley
McFeeley, William S.	Frederick Douglass	1991	1st
McKinney-Whetstone, Diane	Blues Dancing	1999	1st signed
McKinney-Whetstone, Diane	Tempest Rising	1998	1st
McKinney-Whetstone, Diane	Tumbling	1996	1st

McKnight, Reginald	I Get On The Bus	1990 1st
McKnight, Reginald	The Kind of Light That Shines on Texas	1992 1st
McKnight, Reginald	Moustapha's Eclipse	1988 1st
McMillan, Terry (ed.)	Breaking Ice	1990
Meer, Fatima	Higher Than Hope	1988 1st
Mengestu, Dinaw	All Our Names	2014 1st
Mengestu, Dinaw	The Beautiful Things That Heaven Bears	2007 1st
Mengestu, Dinaw	How to Read the Air	2010 1st
Merriwether, Louise	Daddy was a Number Runner	1970 1st
Miller, Wayne F.	Chicago's Southside	2000 1st
Mokgatle, Naboth	The Autobiography of an Unknown South African	1971 1st
Morrison, Toni	Beloved	1987 Galley signe
Morrison, Toni	Home	2012 1st
Morrison, Toni	Jazz	1992 1st
Morrison, Toni	Love	2003 1st signed
Morrison, Toni	A Mercy	2008 1st
Morrison, Toni	Nobel Laureate in Literature 1993	1993
Morrison, Toni	Paradise	1998 1st
Morrison, Toni	Playing in the Dark	1992 1st
Morrison, Toni	Race-ing Justice	1992 1st
Morrison, Toni	Song of Solomon	1977 1st
Morrison, Toni	Tar Baby	1981 1st Trade
Morrison, Toni	What Moves at the Margin	2008 1st
Mosley, Walter	47	2005 1st inscribe
Mosley, Walter	All I Did Was Shoot My Man	2012 1st
Mosley, Walter	Always Outnumbered, Always Outgunned	1998 1st signed
Mosley, Walter	Bad Boy Brawly Brown	2002 1st inscribe
Mosley, Walter	Black Betty	1994 1st
Mosley, Walter	Blonde Faith	2007 1st
Mosley, Walter	Blue Light	1998 1st inscribe
Mosley, Walter	Cinnamon Kiss	2005 1st inscribe
Mosley, Walter	Devil in a Blue Dress	1990 1st
Mosley, Walter	Diablerie	2008 1st
Mosley, Walter	Fear Itself	2003 1st inscribe
Mosley, Walter	Fearless Jones	2001 1st inscribe
Mosley, Walter	Fear of the Dark	2006 1st
Mosley, Walter	Fortunate Son	2006 1st inscribe
Mosley, Walter	Futureland	2001 1st signed
Mosley, Walter	The Gift of Fire	2012 1st
Mosley, Walter	Gone Fishin'	1997 1st inscribe
Mosley, Walter	Known to Evil	2010 1st signed
Mosley, Walter	Last Days of Ptolomy Gray	2010 1st
Mosley, Walter	Little Green	2013 1st signed
Mosley, Walter	Little Scarlet	2004 1st inscribe
Mosley, Walter	A Little Yellow Dog	1996 1st inscribe
Mosley, Walter	The Long Fall	2009 1st signed
Mosley, Walter	The Man In My Basement	2004 1st inscribe
Mosley, Walter	A Red Death	1991 1st signed
Mosley, Walter	RLs Dream	1995 1st inscribe
Mosley, Walter	Rose Gold	2014 1st signed
Mosley, Walter	Six Easy Pieces	2003 1st inscribe
Mosley, Walter	This Year You Write Your Novel	2007 1st inscribe
Mosley, Walter	Walkin' The Dog	1999 1st signed
Mosley, Walter	What Next	2003 1st
Mosley, Walter	When the Thrill is Gone	2011 1st
Mosley, Walter	White Butterfly	1992 1st
Mosley, Walter	Workin' on the Chain Gang	2000 1st
Motley, Willard	Let Noon Be Fair	1966 1st
Motley, Willard	We Fished All Night	1951 1st
Naylor, Gloria	Bailey's Café	1992 1st
Naylor, Gloria	Children of the Night	1995 1st
Naylor, Gloria	Linden Hills	1985 1st
Naylor, Gloria	Mama Day	1988 1st
Naylor, Gloria	The Men of Brewster Place	1998 1st
Neely, Barbara	Blanche Among the Talented Tenth	1994 1st
Neely, Barbara	Blanche Cleans Up	1998 1st
Nelson, Jill	Volunteer Slavery	1993 1st
Nicholas, Denise	Freshwater Road	2005
Norris, Michele	The Grace of Silence	2010 1st
Obama, Barack	The Audacity of Hope	2006 1st signed i
Obama, Barack	Dreams from my Father	1995 1st signed i
Ogletree, Charles	The Presumption of Guilt	2010 1st signed

Okri, Ben	Astonishing The Gods	1995 1st
Okri, Ben	The Famished Road	1991 1st
Okri, Ben	Songs of Enchantment	1993 1st
Okri, Ben	Stars of the New Curfew	1988 1st signed
Organ, Claude	A Century of Black Surgeons Vol 1	1987 1st
Organ, Claude	A Century of Black Surgeons Vol 2	1987 1st
Osekre, Ishmael	Verses for the Masses	2009 signed
Ottley, Roi	A new World A-Coming	1943 2nd
Ottley, Roy	White Marble Lady	1965 1st
Page, Clarence	Showing My Color	1996 1st
Parker, Gwendolyn M.	These Same Long Bones	1994
Parks, Gordon	Half Past Autumn	1997 1st
Parks, Gordon	The Learning Tree	1963 1st signed
Parks, Gordon	Shannon	1981 1st signed
Parks, Gordon	Voices in the Mirror	1990 Galley signe
Pemberton, Gayle	Hottest Water in Chicago	1992
Petry, Ann	The Narrows	1953 1st
Plouffe, David	The Audacity to Win: The Inside Story and Lessons of Barack Obama's H.	2009 signed
Poitier, Sidney	Life Beyond Measure	2008 1st
Poitier, Sidney	The Measure of a Man	2000 1st
Ponder, Rhinold	Wisdom of the Word	1996
Powell, Colin	My American Journey	1995 1st
Proctor, Samuel DeWitt	The Substance of Things Hoped For	1996 1st
Rampersad, Arnold	Jackie Robinson	1997 1st
Reed, Christopher	The Chicago NAACP and the Rise of Black...	1997 1st
Reed, Ishmael	Airing Dirty Laundry	1993 1st signed(?
Reed, Ishmael	Blues City	2003 1st signed
Reed, Ishmael	Flight To Canada	1976 1st
Reed, Ishmael	Japanese by Spring	1993 1st signed
Reed, Ishmael	The Last Days of Lousiana Red	1974 1st
Reed, Ishmael	MultiAmerica	1997 1st
Reed, Ishmael	New and Collected Poems 1964-2006	2006 1st signed
Reed, Ishmael	The Reed Reader	2003 1st signed
Reed, Ishmael	Shrovetide In Old New Orleans	1978 1st
Remnick, David	The Bridge: The Life and Rise of Barack Obama	2010 1st
Ribowsky, Mark	Don't Look Back: Satchel Paige in the Shadows of Baseball	1994
Richardson, Brenda Lane	Chesapeake Song	1993 1st signed
Robinson, Rachel	Jackie Robinson An Intimate Portrait	1996 1st
Rowan, Carl T.	Dream Makers, Dream Breakers	1993 1st
Sampson, Anthony	Mandela	1999
Sapphire	Push	1996 1st
Schomburg Center	New York Pubic Library African American Desk Reference	1999 1st
Schomburg Center	The Black New Yorkers	2000 1st
Schomburg Center	Jubilee	2002 1st
Schulke, Flip	He Had A Dream	1995 1st
Shange, Ntozake	For Colored Girls who have Consdered Suicide When The Rainbow is Enu	1977 1st
Shange, Ntozake	If I Can Cook/You Know God Can	1998 1st
Shange, Ntozake	The Sweet Breath of Lfe	2004 1st
Smith, David James	Young Mandela	2010
Smith, Faye McDonald	Flight of the Blackbird	1996 1st
Smith, Zadie	The Autograph Man	2002 1st signed
Smith, Zadie	Changing My Mind	2009 1st
Smith, Zadie	NW	2012 1st
Smith, Zadie	On Beauty	2005 1st signed
Smith, Zadie	White Teeth	2000 1st signed
Sorin & Shannon	In the Spirit of Martin	2003 1st
Soyinka, Wole	Ake' The Years of Childhood	1981 1st signed
Soyinka, Wole	Art, Dialogue, and Outrage	1993 1st signed
Soyinka, Wole	The Burden of Memory, The Muse of Forgiveness	1999 1st signed
Soyinka, Wole	Isara	1989 1st signed
Soyinka, Wole	You Must Set Forth at Dawn	2006 1st signed
Staples, Brent	Parallel Time	1994 1st
Sterling, Dorothy	We Are Your Sisters	1984 1st
Still, William	Underground Railroad	1970
Stone, David P.	Fallen Prince: William James Edwards	1990 1st inscribe
Stovall, Tyler	Paris Noir	1996 1st
Stowe, Harriet Beecher	Uncle Tom's Cabin	1888 UK Edition
Studio Museum of Harlem	Harlem Renaissance: Art of Black America	1987
Styron, William	The Confessions of Nat Turner	1966 1st
Tademy, Lalita	Cane River	2001 Galley signe
Tademy, Lalita	Citizens Creek	2014 1st signed
Tademy, Lalita	Red River	2007 1st signed

Taulbert, Clifton	The Last Train North	1992 1st
Taulbert, Clifton	Once Upon A Time When We were Colored	1989 1st
Thomas, Sheree	Dark Matter	2000 1st
Thompson, Era Bell	Africa, Land Of My Fathers	1954 1st
Thompson, Era Bell	American Daughter	1946 1st
Thurman, Howard	The Centering Moment	1969 1st
Thurman, Howard	The Creative Encounter	1972
Thurman, Howard	Deep is the Hunger	1996
Thurman, Howard	Deep River	1945 1st
Thurman, Howard	Deep River and the Negro Spiritual Speaks of Life and Death	1990
Thurman, Howard	Disciplines of the Spirit	1987
Thurman, Howard	For the Inward Journey	1984
Thurman, Howard	The Growing Edge	1974
Thurman, Howard	The Inward Journey	1961 1st
Thurman, Howard	The Inward Journey	1990
Thurman, Howard	Jesus and the Disinherited	1981
Thurman, Howard	The Luminous Darkness	1965 1st
Thurman, Howard	Meditations For Apostles of Sensitiveness	1947 1st
Thurman, Howard	Meditations of the Heart	1953 1st
Thurman, Howard	Meditations of the Heart	1992
Thurman, Howard	The Mood of Christmas	1973 1st
Thurman, Howard	The Mood of Christmas	1985
Thurman, Howard	Mysticism and the Experience of Love	1961
Thurman, Howard	The Negro Spiritual Speaks of Life and Death	1947 1st
Thurman, Howard	The Search for Common Ground	1971 1st
Thurman, Howard	A Strange Freedom / ed. By Fluker & Tumber	1998
Thurman, Howard	Temptations of Jesus	1978
Thurman, Howard	With Head and Heart	1979 1st signed
Thurman, Howard and Alfred Fisk	The First Footprints: The Dawn of the Idea of The Church for the Fellows	1975
Townsend, Willa A.	Gospel Pearls	1921 1st
Troupe, Quincy	James baldwin: The Legacy	1989
Truth, Sojourner	Narrative and Book of Life	1970
Tutu, Desmond	The Rainbow People of God	1994 1st
Tye, Larry	Satchel: The Life and Times of an American Legend	2009 1st
Van, Paulina	Regala Healing	2021 1st signed
Van Vechten, Carl	Generations in Black and White	1993
Vanzant, Iyanla	Every Day I Pray	2001
Wade, Brent	Company Man	1992 1st
Wade-Gayles, Gloria	My Soul is a Witness	1995 1st
Walker, Alice	By The Light of My Father's Smile	1998 1st
Walker, Alice	Her Blue Body Everything We know	1991 1st
Walker, Alice	Possessing The Secret Of Joy	1992 1st
Walker, Margaret	Richard Wright: Daemonic Genius	1988
Ward, Samuel Ringgold	Autobiography of a Fugitive Negro	1970
Warren, Gwendolin	Ev'ry Time I Feel The Spirit	1997 1st
Washington, Linn	Black Judges on Justice	1994 1st
Watkins, Mel	Dancing With Strangers	1998 1st
Watkins, Mel	On The Real Side	1994 1st
Wesley, Valerie Wilson	Always True to You in My Fashion	2002 1st
Wesley, Valerie Wilson	Devil's Gonna Get Him	1995
Wesley, Valerie Wilson	Dying in the Dark	2004
Wesley, Valerie Wilson	Easier To Kill	1998
Wesley, Valerie Wilson	No Hiding Place	1997
Wesley, Valerie Wilson	When Death Comes Stealing	1994
Wesley, Valerie Wilson	Where Evil Sleeps	1996
West, Cornel	Brother West: Living and Loving Out Loud	2009 1st signed
West, Cornel	Keeping Faith	1993 1st
West, Cornel	Race Matters	1993 1st
West, Cornel	Restoring Hope	1997 1st
West, Dorothy	The Richer, the Poorer	1995 1st
West, Dorothy	The Wedding	1995 1st
Wheeler, B. Gordon	Black California	1993 1st
Whitehead, Colson	John Henry Days	2001 1st inscribe
Whitehead, Colson	The Noble Hustle	2014 1st signed
Whitehead, Colson	Zone One	2011 1st inscribe
Wideman, John Edgar	The Cattle Killing	1996 1st signed
Wideman, John Edgar	Fanon	2008 1st inscribe
Wideman, John Edgar	Fatheralong	1994 1st
Wideman, John Edgar	Fever	1989 1st
Wideman, John Edgar	Hoop Roots	2001 1st
Wideman, John Edgar	My Soul Has Grown Deep	2001 1st
Wideman, John Edgar	Philadelphia Fire	1990 1st

Wideman, John Edgar	*Reuben*	1987	1st signed
Wideman, John Edgar	*The Stories of John Edgar Wideman*	1992	Galley
Wideman, John Edgar	*Two Cities*	1998	1st
Wilkerson, Isabel	*The Warmth Of Other Suns*	2010	1st inscribe
Williams, Cecil	*No Hiding Place*	1992	1st inscribe
Wilson, William Julius	*When Work Disappears*	1996	1st
Woods, Paula	*Spooks, Spies, and Private Eyes*	1995	1st
Wright, Richard	*American Hunger*	1977	1st
Wright, Richard	*Black Boy*	1945	1st
Wright, Richard	*Black Power*	1954	1st
Wright, Richard	*Eight Men*	1961	1st
Wright, Richard	*Lawd Today*	1963	2nd
Wright, Richard	*The Long Dream*	1958	1st
Wright, Richard	*Native Son*	1940	1st
Wright, Richard	*The Outsider*	1953	1st
Wright, Richard	*Pagan Spain*	1960	1st UK
Wright, Richard	*Rite of Passage*	1994	1st
Wright, Richard	*White Man, Listen!*	1957	1st
Yates, Elizabeth	*Howard Thurman: Portrait of a Political Dreamer*	1964	
Young, Andrew	*An Easy Burden*	1996	1st signed
Young, Andrew	*A Way Out Of No Way*	1994	1st
Zang, David W.	*Fleet Walker's Divided Heart*	1995	

Chapter 11: The Last Mile Foundation

"*I only have a minute. Sixty seconds is it. Forced upon me, I did not choose it. But I know that I must use it, give account if I abuse it, suffer if I lose it. Only a tiny little minute. But eternity is in it.*" *~Dr. Benjamin E. Mays, President, Morehouse College 1940-1970*

Morehouse College

Even as a young boy, the concept of giving back was engrained in me by my mother. As I became successful, I tried to share what I have learned and accumulated. One opportunity arose when my son Jonathan was accepted into Morehouse College in 1996.

Morehouse is an all-male college, founded in 1867, and located in Atlanta Georgia. Its primary purpose is to educate African American young men. Notable graduates include Martin Luther King Jr., Howard Thurman, Benjamin Mays, Samuel L. Jackson, Jeh Johnson, Mordecai Johnson, and Spike Lee.

During Jonathan's freshman year, I was asked to chair the college's parents' council. Historically, many in Morehouse's freshman class were first-generation college students. Because many of these young men did not have a family history attending college, the families either underestimated the cost of college or sent their young men to Morehouse with all the family resources that they could muster and hoped that things would work out.

It was not unusual to see many young men in the registrar's office who could not register for classes because they had miscalculated the cost of their schooling by as little as a few hundred dollars. We decided that when Jonathan graduated and we finished paying his tuition, we would find a way to help these young men.

The Last Mile Foundation – Easing the Way

Establishing, operating, and marketing a foundation is complex. Jane, Kristine and I decided to make the foundation part of our executive search firm, Grisham Group Executive Search. We were going to call it an educational foundation, until our close friend and former classmate at DePaul, John Peck, gave us a better idea.

He knew that we wanted to start a foundation to help young, first-generation African American students complete their first-year financial requirements and successfully enter college. John said, "Everyone seems to have a scholarship foundation. Why not make yours different? Why don't you start a last dollar foundation and call it the Last Mile Foundation because you are helping students reach *the last mile*?" Thus the Last Mile Foundation was born.

John and his wife, Barbara, are additional examples of lifetime friendships that have positively influenced me through their example. When your friends consistently make good decisions and are successful, you want to make good decisions and have an opportunity to be successful.

I met John when we were freshmen at DePaul, and I met Barbara when we were teenagers, attending Gorham United Methodist Church on the Southside of Chicago. Both John and Barbara grew up in working-class homes, graduated from DePaul with degrees in accounting, and both became CPAs. John rose to the partnership level at Ernst and Young, one of the Big 4 CPA firms, and Barbara held a number of positions, including Managing Deputy Controller for the City of Chicago, CFO for Chicago Board of Education and professor of accounting at the University of Illinois, Chicago Campus.

To operate and market our foundation, we formed a relationship with the East Bay Community Fund in Oakland. One criterion that a student had to satisfy to qualify for funding was to write an essay on the following topic: *What is your big dream and how do you change the world and how are the two related?* We wanted to change and expand the thinking of our young scholars. We did not realize that the essays would be so powerful that they would change us.

These are two of our favorite essays and one poem.

The No Child Essay
by Mary Shodiya

Having survived more at nineteen than most are forced to endure in an entire lifetime, I look back at the road I have tread thus far and all along the tortuous path see the pieces of my dream that when assembled form a formidable dream. For some dreams are made of grandiose visions of what the world ought to be, but for this young woman my dreams are made of my absolute certainty of what the world ought not to be.

I was born and raised in Nigeria, a nation that has proven not only incapable of educating its youth, but unfailingly entangles them in the chains of poverty. I was fortunate enough to be one of the blessed few that escaped. Of my escape and the nightmarish burdens that accompany the blessing of being an immigrant in the United States has been borne the absolute conviction that no child's destiny should be determined or impeded by the circumstances of his or her birth.

No child should be forced to abandon their homeland and in so doing all that they have ever known and loved on the quest for success. No child should have to become an adult before they have exhausted the wonders of childhood. No child should have to give up their birthright in one nation to become one of the immigrant masses in another without the exact same rights and privileges as the natives.

When I ponder the path, the world has forced upon me, I see the gaping holes through which I should have fallen into obscurity and mediocrity save for the absolute grace of God Almighty. And I find myself irate at the thought of the unimaginable number of brilliant souls that have been lost to the world as a result of all the cracks, crevices, gorges and craters on the path to success.

I don't know when or how, but I have come to the absolute utter irrevocable determination to do whatsoever is within my power so that no child will have to endure the torturous trials and tribulations that constitute the tale of my life, that no child will ever have to tumble into the holes I narrowly escaped into the abyss of failure thus depriving the world of their incredible intellectual potential, every ounce of which the world is in dire need of.

I envision myself founding a comprehensive non-profit organization whose primary mission will be to strive to safeguard as many children as humanly possible from the pitfalls along the path to success that almost managed to extinguish my future and to ensure that those very same children enjoy the numerous gifts that life has to offer that I was deprived of and to write for each of them a success story of which fairy tales are made.

Pragmatically put, my non-profit organization will seek to share the wealth that is Africa – its majestic landscape, wildlife, and magnificent tribes of humanity, not to mention its glorious heritage that will inspire every emotion known to man. So that the new generation might gain character, strength, love of country and inspiration – just some of the countless ingredients in the recipe for success. It is in having seen the marvels of Africa and having experienced the magnificence of its people that Africa's youth will gain the will to preserve her for all the ages through whatever means necessary.

My non-profit will also strive to share the wealth of knowledge comprised from the millions of African men and women who like me have been forced to seek our fortune on shores leagues away from home so that those who follow our footsteps will steer well away from all the pitfalls we've encountered on our respective journeys towards our respective destinies. This means educating those families who choose to send their little ones abroad about the immigration process and what to expect in the process of assimilation so that their sacrifices are as meaningful as possible.

For one thing, they would be able to avoid the tragedy of sending children abroad for an education on a tourist visa which literally creates huge gaping holes in the educational system for that child. And my organization would provide post-immigration support for these families and their children throughout the process of assimilation.

Simply put, my non-profit organization will ensure that the majestic magnificence that is Africa will be imprinted in the hearts of these children as we provide them with every resource necessary from legal advice to human resources to ensure a most successful and productive immigration which is a necessary service while our organization works on developing a stable educational infrastructure within Africa and a general environment that will be able to provide our children with futures awash with possibilities.

Compressed further, the non-profit organization I shall establish will seek to straighten, shore up and fail proof the torturous terrain to success that the African Child at this point in time is finding virtually impossible to navigate. And in so doing, I hope to force progress in this world by ensuring more soldiers to fight the battle and commanders to win the war one brilliant child at a time.

The Born in Prison Essay
(Name Confidential)

My life is filled with many spontaneous dreams; however, I am focused on one particular dream, which is to graduate from college. I knew it was imperative for this dream to become a reality because of the conditions in which I was raised. Growing up in the inner-city ghettos of San Francisco California, I along with my peers became exposed to alcohol, drugs and crime.

I witnessed many African American males in my community, including my father, leave home and go off to prison. I knew growing up that this was a false perception of reality for young Black males such as me, and that the examples set before me were negative because those particular individuals allowed their circumstances to dictate their behavior. As such, I battled with many different issues of my own while growing up, which almost allowed my dreams to become deferred.

First, I was born in a California State Prison Women's Correctional Facility, and I was immediately taken from my mother at birth. I grew up in many foster homes and was informed by the system that I was slower than the other children who were my age, and I would struggle to keep up in school.

However, I knew inside that I was a smart and intelligent person and was capable of achieving anything I set my mind to. I also understood that my determination to become successful was not enough and that I needed strong rules for living that would help shape my dreams. I first had to deal with my personal anger, fear and pain, which resulted from never knowing my real father.

Dealing with the understanding that I was considered a drug addicted baby by the system, and not having a mother to care for me was difficult, and at times a struggle for me. Therefore, much like the influences I studied while growing up, I started to become just like them.

My dream of attending college and graduating was slowly expiring. I was rarely exposed to anything positive and uplifting besides church, and even there the preacher was not informing the congregation about the need for higher education amongst black men and women in the community. I knew that education was the only way I could better myself and those around me.

I found the Omega Boys Club in San Francisco California during the spring semester of my sophomore year in high school, and they informed me that through hard work and dealing with my personal issues that I would be able to attend college.

Today, I am a transfer student at the University of Memphis majoring in Education with a concentration in creative writing. It is because of God that I am able to fulfill this dream, and he has carried me through many trials and tribulations throughout my life in order for this to be possible.

I now understand through my rigorous college experience that I am compelled to lead a life of service in my community, now and after I receive my degree. I truly did not choose education but rather education chose me! Thus, I realize the need for more male teachers, particularly Black male teachers in America and the impact that I can have on a child's life by being a teacher and a positive role model.

I do not believe I can single handedly change the world by myself, but I am convinced that I am helping to change the world at this moment by changing myself. I once studied an author by the name of Herman Melville who wrote, "For it is better to fail as an original than to succeed as an imitation." That statement is true for me as I continue to strive to be the difference in my community and the world.

My dream will help keep young people such as myself alive and free of incarceration. I want to develop a curriculum in high schools that will teach life skills and self-education. I believe teaching people about themselves is essential for reaching their dreams. I think becoming something other than an entertainer or a professional athlete is important for young people growing up to see in the community.

Nonetheless, my dream can never be truly fulfilled until all of humanity discovers who they truly are. As Martin Luther King Jr. stated, "We are all caught in an inescapable web of mutuality; whatever affects one directly affects all indirectly, for I can never be what I ought to be, until you are what you ought to be, and you can never be who you ought to be, until I am who I ought to be."

Therefore, the two questions, "What is your dream and how will you change the world?" are directly related because the ability to dream must be driven by one's ability to achieve. In closing, I would like to thank the Last Mile Foundation for this opportunity to be a voice for young people who have had similar experiences, such as me growing up and who have overcome their circumstances in order to lead positive lives.

Never Again by Ishmael Osekre

NEVER AGAIN

No more pair to tear
or be in haste to hate
or be quick to prick
hearts to hurt
and cause despair without repair
and destroy lives and not ask why.
No more hold on to the initials and the superficials
and exchange the essentials for the diferentials.
thinking we will be medicated while we are desiccated.
Never again.
Never again must seeds be sown amongst weeds,
neither must vines not be planted in their time
nor jewels be extracted without expecting the duels.
Never again
Never again must the day be a drain
and the way be lay
and chances be treated with glances
and fortunes be called misfortunes by us.
Never again.
Never again must our light be hidden from sight
and our might turn to blight
because of lack of might, sight and insight.
Never again
Never again must we be denied of our portion and our potion
and our position in our disposition under the dispensations
until we are denied of our blessing and lifting and progressing
and are left as defts in debts. Never again.
Never again must we trip or be stripped
until we slip the cup from the lip
and roll into social, economical, psychological and spiritual
bankruptcy.
Never again.

Never again must we continue in the ashes and mashes and
stashes of acrimony and tyranny
nor in anomalies, abnormalities and delinquencies
that impairs the mind
and tears the heart
and disturbs our spirit,
denying us of our gratitude for the past
our attitude in the present
and our latitude in the future.
All eyes 're on you.
All eyes are on us.
The seas and the seeds,
the shadows in the gallows,
the marrows in the hollows
and the arrows in the fallows
are sitting in the waiting
and waiting for the lifting
and the lifting of your gifting.
All eyes are on us
for you to make a mark
positively deep enough
for the earth to know
when you are gone.
Never again.

Osekre

Alive and Free/Omega Boys Club

During "The Great Recession" The Last Mile Foundation's golf tournament moved from the East Bay Community Foundation and became a fund-raising arm of "Alive and Free". Founded by Dr Joe Marshall 36 years ago, its mission is to "keep young people alive and free, unharmed by violence and free from incarceration."

Proceeds from the golf tournament primarily fund college scholarships for students that complete "Alive and Free's program. Hundreds of students have received financial assistance from "Alive and Free" to finance their college education.

Godspeed, Miss Jane

Last Mile, and the students we were able to help became very special to us. Some of the associations and friendships have lasted. My family and I were especially moved by the tribute written by the volunteers at our annual fund-raising golf tournament. It appeared in a tournament brochure.

GODSPEED, MISS JANE

As you may have already noticed, our golf tournament volunteer team has been forever changed.

On January 9th of this year, our friend and colleague, Mrs. Jane Grisham, beloved wife of our tournament chairperson, Arnold Grisham, was called home to be with our Lord.

Jane was a scholar, teacher, mentor and philanthropist. She taught third grade for over 35 years. She taught long enough to teach the children of some of her earlier students. She made close friends of many of her colleagues while educating young people from disadvantaged backgrounds.

Jane's legacy is one of taking God's gifts to her and making them available to others. She will be fondly remembered for her big smile, her soft spoken and understanding ways, a quiet yet sharp wit, and her accessible presence that was always available to anyone in need.

Among the activities that Jane was most proud of is the Last Mile Foundation that she and Arnold founded more than ten years ago. It is the fundraising arm of Alive & Free-Omega Boys Club and it is the very reason for which we are all here today.

Jane will be thought of warmly by those of us who had the pleasure of striking up a conversation with her at a previous golf tournament; perhaps while laughing at ourselves because of a bogey or a missed putt, or while keeping an eye on a favorite item in the silent auction.

Forever in our hearts, she will be remembered simply as "Miss Jane," the beautiful, kind lady who made us all feel welcomed and appreciated, as we played our part during this great day of golf with a greater purpose.

Godspeed, Miss Jane.

Chapter 12: Paulina Rosa Van

"When you know, you know." - Unknown

One of the things that I learned quickly after Jane died, was that I could not live happily without a woman in my life and I lived to share my life with a woman. Without a woman as a life mate, I am missing a major life purpose. Having a mother who thought that butter did not melt in my mouth caused me to love and revere women. I knew that I wanted to remarry, and I had a list of what I was looking for in a mate:

- Christian
- Democrat
- Lived through personal suffering

- A person who was navigating this world on her own steam

I did not realize that there was an "it" factor that you cannot explain. A person who, when you are with them, time passes quickly. Paulina Rosa Van is that person.

When two highly educated people marry at age 22, you and your mate have a lifetime of growth and self-discovery. When you marry at 72 and your wife is 65, and you both have had long careers of increasing achievement, that discovery happens at warp speed.

Instead of retiring, you begin to look at each other's professional platform through the other's unique lens, honed over decades of achievement and struggle, and begin to give each other suggestions of how the other can continue and enhance their work. Professionally, as your paths intersect, you begin to vibrate at the same level.

An example is *Regala Healing*, a book of poems written by Paulina that has taken us both on its own journey. Paulina is an intuit and a Reiki master. Reiki is an energy healing technique that promotes physical and emotional healing, brings on relaxation, and reduces stress and anxiety.

Paulina – The Early Years

Paulina was born in Panama on June 13, 1953, to Paul Trotman and Una Davis. Paulina's father enlisted in the United States Army and served in Korea during the Korean War. He was discharged in New York in the mid-1950s, remained in the U.S., and became a U.S. citizen. He had the foresight and vision to use his military wartime credentials to help Una, Paulina, and his extended family to migrate to the U.S. shortly after his discharge.

Paul and Una were professionals in Panama. Paul was in the dental field but in the U.S., became a computer specialist working for the U.S. government in Washington D.C. Una was an accountant in Panama and, in the U.S., started as a teller at a bank in Brooklyn. She soon rose to loan officer.

While Paulina was born in Panama, her younger brother, Michael, was born in the U.S. During their marriage Paul and Una did not share a home. Una was the sole supporter of her children and her mother. Paulina and her two siblings spent much of their childhood hungry and without proper clothing. Una's personal ethic meant accepting governmental assistance was never an option. She valued education and therefore sacrifices were made so that her children could attend private schools.

In the late 1960s, Una relocated the family to San Francisco, California, to explore new personal employment and educational opportunities for her children. The change of coasts did not change the family's economic situation. Una was still the head of the household and with much commitment, grit, and love provided for her family.

About the scholar/artist
Paulina Van, PhD, RN, CNE

Dr. Paulina Van entered academia after spending over twenty years in various executive-level positions in acute care, home care, and public health. She has held faculty or administrative positions in the Schools of Nursing at Samuel Merritt University (current), the University of San Francisco, the University of California, San Francisco, and California State University, East Bay (CSUEB) teaching at the doctoral, masters, and baccalaureate levels. She is currently working as a professor and researcher at Samuel Merritt University.

Dr. Van graduated with a Baccalaureate degree in Nursing from the University of San Francisco. She earned a master's degree in nursing administration, a Doctor of Philosophy in Nursing degree and a Postdoctoral Fellowship from the University of California, San Francisco. She has also earned the designation Certified Nurse Educator (CNE) from the National League for Nursing. Dr. Van holds five additional distinguished certifications: Certified Instructor, Online Teaching & Learning (California State University, East Bay), Certified Mediator (The Center for Narrative and Discursive Practice), Reiki Master, HeartMath® Certified Trainer (HeartMath Institute), and Caritas® Coach (Watson Caring Science Institute).

Dr. Van chaired twelve DNP Project Committees between 2015-2020. She continues to support DNP students in this role as well as teach various DNP theory courses. Dr. Van also teaches in nursing pre licensure programs.

Her course load has included theory courses in research, leadership, introduction to nursing, and death and dying and clinical courses in community/mental health and senior synthesis/capstone. In her quest to continue to bring the latest technological advances to student learning activities, she constructed [supported by instructional designers] various multimedia projects using interactive visuals and quality audio. These learning objects were incorporated into selected graduate or undergraduate nursing research, education innovation, leadership, and general education courses.

Dr. Van is passionate about her program of research, which began in 1996 and is focused on the wide range of issues concerning women and pregnancy loss. This passion began with a focus on African American women and has extended to diverse women in the US and internationally in Mexico and Spain.

Besides publications and presentations, a significant contribution to practice has been her development and dissemination of an emerging theoretical Model of Coping after Pregnancy Loss for Diverse Women. She has presented papers on these topics in the United States Canada, Columbia, Egypt, England, Greece, Italy, Mexico, and Thailand to multidisciplinary audiences of health care professionals.

Dr. Van earned research funding awards from various organizations, including the National Institute of Health,

*National Institute of Nursing Research, Johnsons & Johnson,
Sigma Theta Tau, University of California, San Francisco.*

*Beginning in 2014, Dr. Van introduced meditation and
mindfulness activities to nursing students during on-ground
class sessions to positively influence their learning
experiences and overall academic performance. The results
were so powerful that in 2017 she created online modules to
provide similar experiences to doctoral students. The results
of her initial work were recently published, and results from
the online project are being developed for publication.*

*Dr. Van's most recent grant award is for the HRSA,
Nursing Education Opportunity Program, Nursing
Workforce Diversity Program (#1 D19HP31820-01-00). This
3- year grant award ($1,500,000.00) provided for the
recruitment, retention, and graduation of African American
and Latino nursing students to enhance the number of
registered nurses available to work in the diverse San
Francisco/Bay Area communities.*

*The various interventions are evidence-based and
delivered by a diverse team of interdisciplinary
professionals.*

Paulina – Nursing

Paulina worked hard to excel academically. She was a
valedictorian candidate at the University of San Francisco. She
became Merritt Hospital's youngest nurse executive and, to date
(2023), is still the only person of African or Hispanic descent to hold
that position. She earned her MS and PhD in nursing at the University
of California, San Francisco. Her research focused on developing
coping and healing strategies for diverse women after pregnancy
loss.

Paulina has been invited to speak about her research at numerous
conferences all over the world. One of the plans for our marriage was
that I would accompany her to these conferences, and we would plan
a vacation near the locale after the conference ended.

Our first conference was in London, and we cruised up the Danube following the conference. Our second conference was to be in Lisbon, Portugal and we were going to take a cruise along the Douro, but COVID began to surge, and the conference was cancelled. We are looking forward to continuing this part of our journey as the virus subsides.

American Academy of Nursing

While this book was being written, Paulina received the highest honor a nurse leader and educator can receive for a lifetime of contributions and impact in the nursing profession. On October 7, 2023, Paulina was inducted as a Fellow in the American Academy of Nursing, during the organization's 2023 Health Policy Conference,

Celebrating 50 Years of Leadership, Policy, and Partnerships in Washington DC.

The Academy is the world's premier nursing organization. She is one of 253 distinguished nurse leaders and educators in the 2023 class of Fellows. Worldwide there are 28 million registered nurses, four million are in the US. Paulina joins an elite group of only 3000 Fellows.

American Academy of Nursing Announces the 2023 Class of New Fellows
Academy to Induct 253 Nurse Leaders in Its 50th Anniversary Year

June 28, 2023 (Washington, DC) — The American Academy of Nursing (Academy) announces today that it will induct 253 distinguished nurse leaders into the 2023 Class of Fellows. The inductees will be recognized for their substantial, sustained, and outstanding impact on health and health care at the Academy's annual Health Policy Conference, taking place on October 5 – 7, 2023 in Washington, DC. This year's conference theme is *"Celebrating 50 Years of Leadership, Policy, and Partnership."*

The newest Fellows, and largest class, represent 40 states, the District of Columbia, and 13 countries. In welcoming these Fellows, the Academy will be comprised of more than 3,000 leaders who are experts in policy, research, administration, practice, and academia that champion health and wellness, locally and globally.

"As the American Academy of Nursing's President, it gives me great pride to welcome these incredible leaders into our organization during our 50th anniversary year. Reflecting on the Academy's history, we began with 36 Charter Fellows in 1973 who saw the need for an organization that would recognize and elevate the impact of nursing on health care," said Kenneth R. White, PhD, RN, AGACNP, ACHPN, FACHE, FAAN. "The Academy continues to convene and celebrate nurses who make extraordinary contributions to improve health through the generation, synthesis, and dissemination of nursing knowledge. This year's group of inductees truly represents today's thought leaders and the diversity of our profession's policy leaders, practitioners, educators, and innovators. Each Fellow of the Academy is changing the future of health and health care through their support to advance equity, promote inclusion, and lift up the next generation of nurses, advancing the Academy's vision of healthy lives for all people."

The 2023 Class of Fellows represents nursing's positive impact through representation in a variety of roles and settings from governmental positions to executive and entrepreneurial leadership in practice, non-profits, as well as higher education.

Through a rigorous and competitive application process, the Academy's <u>Fellow Selection Committee</u>, which is comprised of elected and appointed Fellows, reviewed nearly 400 applications, ultimately selecting the 2023 Fellows based on their contributions to advance the public's health. Induction into the Academy is a significant milestone in which past and current accomplishments are honored by their colleagues within and outside the profession.

The Academy is thrilled to host the Induction Ceremony and Soiree on the evening of Saturday, October 7, 2023. The program will feature short, personalized videos from each inductee on the impact they have made to advance health. This event is a special tribute to nursing leadership, research, and innovation where colleagues, family, friends, and sponsors can gather together in Washington, DC to celebrate the power of nursing's impact. <u>Learn more</u> about the Academy and v<u>isit the policy conference</u> website for more details.

"Royal Order of the Tiger and Hawk"

Paulina's professional research has been focused on women who have experienced involuntary pregnancy loss and how they coped with this tragedy. On July 13, 2023, that work was recognized by an important group in Ghana, West Africa.

The maternal and infant mortality rate in Ghana has been among the highest in West Africa. Paulina's research and contributions to promoting the health of mothers and their babies are known worldwide. Because of that, the subnational monarchy of Ghana, a group of elders regarded as custodians of tradition, health, and culture, elevated Paulina to be *The Honorable Grand Dame* of the *Royal Order of the Tiger and Hawk.*

Regala Healing

So much of Paulina's healing expertise and energy is revealed in the summary of her work detailed below in Nursology, an online platform for professional nurses. Below is the first article published to promote Paulina's esthetic healing work on the website https://nursology.net/patterns-of-knowing-in-nursing/aesthetic-knowing/paulina-van-poetry/

Paulina Van: Lyrical Poetry/Regalos

Live and Love Again

A "Caritas Coach® is defined as a knowledgeable, experienced, reflective health care professional, who is prepared and committed to personally and professionally practice and model intelligent heart-centered approaches to health care by translating and sustaining the ethic, philosophy, theory, and practice of the Science of Human Caring into our systems and society." [1] Here, I give you a glimpse of how Caritas Coach® education experiences were an element that transformed me into being and becoming a giver of gifts for you and myself.

"I get to live and love again" is the last line of my first lyrical poem. That writing experience opened the flood gates of self-love, self-care, self-acceptance, and ultimately healing. I pondered an explanation for my transcendence: Was it the voice of the traumatized child within me? Was it the focus on self-love and self-care during my Caritas Coach® education journey or the promptings from my instructor to get out of my head and into my heart? Was it my daily meditation and gratitude journaling? Was it the love and caring from my new husband? Was it my brief guided expressive writing experience during a workshop with young African American female entrepreneurs? Was it my longing for a happy, healthy life? Was it the desire to be free of the constant

fear (a reality from my childhood) of being hungry again? Was it the voices of those who passed on before me, letting me know of the hope and joy I could embrace? Was it the power of my Creator making His presence immutable?

I believe it was a little of each life experience which led to my expanded consciousness and the creation of over 100 healing narratives that took on the form of lyrical poetry. A loved one's response to my writings was that 'they were given to me and now I must give it to the world.' These words led me to entitle my lyrical poems regalos—the Spanish translation of gifts.

These regalos represent my Hispanic heritage and describe the channeling, downloads, nonconscious states during which these regalos immerged from within me. Each regalo reflects a unique glimpse of my life story. Each emits the power and energy of love, kindness, compassion, acceptance, self-love, self-care, resilience, forgiveness and is inspiring, transformative, centering, and calming.

A recent chat with Dr. Chinn gave me the courage and platform to share what I believe may potentiate your healing as it has mine. How might you use each of these regalos? Perhaps as a morning or nighttime readings or devotions, meditation/mindfulness focus, an afternoon reading to refocus, relax, reenergize, or as a centering guide before an individual or group session with colleagues or students.

This collection of regalos will be available in a book scheduled for publication later in 2021.

With my open, loving heart, I share two of my regalos. I look forward to your comments as you experience your journey with them.

"Touched"

I was touched
While teaching about death
I was touched
And had to take a breath
I was touched
By students vulnerability
I was touched
With their sensitivity
I was touched
And paid attention
I was touched
And made mention
I was touched
Their faces told it all
I was touched
Their words made me bawl
I was touched
Experiencing their transformation
I was touched
By their transcendence and formation
I was touched
Having entrée into the depths of their
Thoughts and feelings
I was touched
My students gave their lives new meanings.

©2021 Paulina Van

"Happy Today"

I'm happy today
I made myself sleep in
I'm happy today
There's a sense of calm within

I'm happy today
Smiling, just because
I'm happy today
And living life with gusto and applause
I'm happy today
Facing unexpected opportunity
I'm happy today
Embracing my immense ingenuity
I'm happy today
Burdens are lifting
I'm happy today
No more weightlifting
I'm happy today
Reflecting on my vow
I'm happy today
In the here and now.

© 2021 Paulina Van

Paulina's 100 poems in her book, *Regalo Healing*, are inspired…
literally. Paulina never read, liked or owned poetry books before
writing these poems. This is how it often happens. We could be
eating dinner or relaxing, or she could be in the shower, and a warm
feeling would envelop her. She would quickly go to her computer
and receive an awareness from God that would be a fully formed
poem.

Almost all the poems have an anaphorical structure and a few use
words unfamiliar to her. But when she looked up the word, it fits the
poem. The length of most of the poems fit classical 9-12-24- and 36-
line lengths. Every poem is about her healing transcendence from the
past. She received another message from our Maker that told her
when Regala Healing was finished.

The poems did not stop when we self-published *Regala Healing*
in September 2021. Paulina has completed four more books
consisting of a few hundred poems that move from the past and looks
at a hopeful future. It is noteworthy that the awareness of new poems
continues to come to her.

Since November 2021 she hosts a biweekly Sunday online show
on blackdoctor.org, where she discusses poetry, healing, meditation,
and other related topics. Her library of Sunday shows and book
signings can be viewed on her website, regalahealing.com.

Paulina has recently established *The Gift of Healing Foundation* with the following mission and vision:

Mission

The mission of *The Gift of Healing Foundation* is to foster a heart-centered, compassionate community dedicated to promoting healing and well-being through the integration of mindfulness, meditation, poetry, and other healing arts. Our mission is to create a safe, inclusive space where individuals can connect, learn, and grow in their personal journey toward wellness.

We strive to empower individuals with the knowledge, tools, and resources needed to cultivate a deep sense of self-care, compassion, and love for themselves and others. Our goal is to make a positive impact in the world by promoting healing and resilience through the transformative power of the arts and mindful practices.

Vision

The Gift of Healing Foundation envisions a world where every individual is empowered to embrace their own unique journey toward healing and well-being. We strive to create a heart-centered, compassionate community that celebrates the transformative power of poetry, mindfulness, meditation, and the healing arts. Our vision is to build a sense of belonging and connectedness among individuals, regardless of their backgrounds or life experiences.

We believe that by promoting love, caring, and compassion towards oneself and others, we can create a world where all individuals are free to thrive and flourish. Our goal is to inspire and empower individuals to cultivate a deep sense of inner peace, resilience, and joy while promoting a culture of healing and well-being in our communities and beyond.

Some of the most popular poems:

"In This Moment"

In this moment
I reflect on my life
In this moment
Everything is alright
In this moment
Somethings rising within
In this moment
It's everywhere I've been
In this moment
I feel an embrace
In this moment
It's all about God's grace.
© 2021 Paulina Van

"Being Vulnerable"

Being vulnerable
Is frightening
Being vulnerable
Is enlightening
Being vulnerable
Draws others near
Being vulnerable
Creates fear
Being vulnerable
Transforms my thinking
Being vulnerable
Gives me an inkling
Being vulnerable
Is living
Being vulnerable
Creates giving
Being vulnerable

Is churning within
Being vulnerable
Is how I win.
© 2021 Paulina Van

"It's Amazing"

It's amazing
To be filled with grace
It's amazing
To have won the race
It's amazing
The flow of my life
It's amazing
I've lost the strife
It's amazing
So bright is my aura
Radiating from my soul
Letting me know
I am amazing.
© 2021 Paulina Van

The main thing is keeping the main thing the main thing.

Four books later, one of her poems resonated with my professional life. Many companies have sayings or phrases that capture the culture or "work ethic" of the organization. In a commercial banking group, line officers will typically have numerous competing tasks on their desks that need to be handled, completed, or resolved.

Lou Cosso was one of my bosses at Wells Fargo who, as I said earlier, became one of my closest friends. Lou was famous for saying, "The main thing is keeping the main thing the main thing." I was sitting at the kitchen table talking to Lou on a speaker phone and we were reminiscing and laughing about "keeping the main thing the main thing." Paulina passed by and the next thing I knew, she had written a poem about "the main thing."

A couple of weeks later, a financial institution where I was a consultant asked me to prepare a relevant and timely speech for their credit group. Since keeping the main thing, the main thing was top of mind because of my discussions with Lou and Paulina, I mentioned Paulina's poem in my speech.

Within the group, the poem took on a life of its own and bookmarks were prepared for the troops (see below). Paulina copyrighted the poem, and it is now in its second printing.

One of the credit analysts wrote the following:

"Please let Paulina know – I loved it so much that I printed it out and hung it in my cubicle! What a great reminder to look at every day – and remember that 'the main thing – is to keep the main thing, the main thing.'"

Angelica Milea Van

God chooses our parents and our children. Occasionally in a lifetime, God gives us the opportunity to participate in the choosing. When Paulina and I decided to marry, Angelica and I decided to choose each other as a new father and daughter.

Angelica decided during her college years that she would live her life in Los Angeles. During her early formative years, she knew her calling would be in the fashion and esthetics world, and she has become very successful, developing a reputation as a talented executive who has a special gift for her crafts.

Angelica has a very kind spirit and practical sensibility. She has been a great sounding board for her mother over the years, and as our relationship deepens, I am learning to seek her counsel also.

Arnold and Paulina

Chapter 13: The Way Continues

"Let us live so that when we come to die even the undertaker will be sorry." ~Mark Twain

Paulina and I have been blessed to have two residences, a primary home east of Sacramento, California, and a pied-a-terre in northern California's East Bay. On Sunday, June 14, 2022, I was driving on the freeway at about 65 miles per hour with an 18-wheeler behind me. Suddenly, I experienced a visual *whiteout.* Everything in my sight became white for five seconds. I subsequently learned from my doctor, Dr. Rollington Ferguson, who as I mentioned earlier is usually the smartest guy in the room, that I had a Transient Ischemic Attack or TIA, a so-called mini stroke. The cause was a decreased blood flow to my brain.

So, what caused the TIA? Dr. Ferguson admitted me into Summit Hospital in Oakland, California, where I was given what seemed like an endless number of tests. I have a Boston Scientific Pacemaker because I have longer than normal pauses between heartbeats. Every six months, I see a Boston Scientific representative who, wirelessly, uploads every heartbeat I have had since the last transmission to his computer. On this day, he was summoned to my bedside and saw that I had an atrial fibrillation or AFib moment at the exact time of my TIA.

So now, what caused my AFib? The medical community does not seem to be able to identify a definitive cause, but I am told that taking a blood thinner can reduce the probability of a reoccurrence.

I believe that there are four factors that may have converged to create the "perfect storm" that caused my AFib. They are as follows:

1. The probability of experiencing AFib increases as we age. I am 76 and I have been transparent and candid with my community, most of whom are over 60 about what happened to me. I have learned that a full 20% of people that know about my atrial fibrillation have told me that they have had AFib experiences.

2. I was dehydrated. Friends flew to San Francisco to see the 5th Golden State Warrior playoff game and before the game we had wine at a sunny and warm outdoor Tiburon venue before the game.

3. I had just recovered from COVID, and some have associated COVID and COVID vaccinations with strokes. African Americans may be at greater risk.

4. I had recently allowed myself to experience stress in ways that could have been avoided.

So what is the point of this story? First, in the medical community, I am a unicorn. My wife is a PhD nurse educator. My doctor, Dr. Rollington Ferguson, is a Black man, with two specialties (cardiology and internal medicine). And I am covered by three medical insurances. I was admitted to a hospital, diagnosed, and treated very quickly. On average, White men live 10 years longer than Black men. One reason is, most Black men do not have my kind of rapid response medical team that I have when faced with an existential medical event.

Second, as I said in my preface, we need to tell our story while we can because we never know when we have said our last prayer or had our last meal, and on I-80 on June 14, 2022, I had a moment when I thought that day was my judgment day and I had said my last prayer and had my last meal.

So why am I still here? My Creator has given me more than the biblical promise in Psalm 90 (threescore and ten). I had the best first wife that a poor boy from the South Side of Chicago could have imagined. Now I have been given the best second wife, who has tremendous skills, and together we are learning that our skills complement each other and allow us to be of service to our communities in ways we could not have imagined before we met.

I am blessed because I no longer have a boss or a schedule, but I am driven to work every day because I know on judgment day I will be asked, "What did you do with all that was given to you?" I know whatever answer I give will be insufficient, but hopefully my Creator will say, to paraphrase Timothy 4:7-8, "He fought a good fight, he finished the race, and he kept the faith."

I have a community of people running alongside me. They know who they are. I would like to thank them for allowing me to join them as part of our collective journeys. They are big thinkers, truth tellers, and connectors, and we all hope one day our creator will say we fought a good fight, we finished the race, and we kept the faith. Until that judgment day, I will continue to believe that the "book of my life" is still being written and my "best days are ahead of me."

The Good Lord willing,

I still have some life to live,

I still have some stuff to do,

And I still have mountains to climb and rivers to cross.

ATG

Epilogue

Making a way out of no way
- an African American expression

My life has been a study in making a way out of no way. I made a way out of no way when my father lost his job and I had to figure out how to complete my education.

I made a way out of no way by getting a DePaul University BS and MBA that gave me the confidence and credentials to become one of the first generation of African American business executives to enter an unwelcoming and unfriendly world. I made a way out of no way when I was stopped at every turn by institutional racism in 1970s Chicago as I tried to navigate a banking career and moved to California with Wells Fargo.

I made a way out of no way as my family adjusted to the increased cost of living in California as we worked to create a better life for ourselves. I made a way out of no way as I navigated through my impostor syndrome and survivor guilt as Wells Fargo had more confidence in my abilities than I did.

I made a way out of no way by starting a bank and saving another bank from failing and thereby creating opportunities for others and myself. I made a way out of no way as my family suffered through losing the glue that held us together, the loss of Jane. I made a way out of no way as I redoubled my efforts in being a service to others as I dealt with new survivor guilt in outliving Jane.

And finally, I made a way out of no way in marrying Paulina, who has given me new purpose and has enriched my life through her academic and personal journey to help others.

Because "what's past is prologue," I am confident that, if necessary, I can continue make a way out of no way, because my journey continues. And it makes me so proud to see how that journey, that way, has been passed on. My 19-year-old granddaughter who seemingly as she came out of the womb, was wise beyond her years, has been a driven, focused and intense person.

She is now enrolled at UCLA. She recently said to me before reading my epilogue, *"Can I tell you a secret, Grandpa? At first, I just had a will, but I didn't see a way. Then I willed myself into a way, and now there is a way."*

Where there is a will, there is a way - Bailey Holliman

Again, I hope that what I have written will be helpful to a few people.

Arnold T. Grisham

Arnold Grisham's Profile

Printed in the USA
CPSIA information can be obtained
at www.ICGtesting.com
LVHW022057181223
766831LV00023B/165/J